THE JOURNEY FROM ABANDONMENT TO HEALING 2.0

© Copyright 2020 by SCOTT J. PINE

First Edition: October 2020

Cover: Illustration made by Diego Gilmar Valenzuela Astudillo

Printed in the United States of America

SCOTT J. PINE

THE JOURNEY FROM ABANDONMENT TO HEALING 2.0

My Heart Hurts!

AN ASTOUNDING GUIDE

To Healing and
the Grief Cure for the Loss of Love.
Surviving Through and Recovering from the
Five Stages that Accompany the Loss of Love
to Feel Better Immediately and
Rebuild YourLife

TABLE OF CONTENTS

Dedicated to all my friends and to all the people
who gave me their help.
Thanks a lot!
Thanks to all of you for your confidence
in my qualities and what I do.
Scott J. Pine

INTRODUCTION

What is abandonment?" people ask. "Is it about people in search of their mothers? Or people left on someone else's doorstep as children?"

My answer is that every day there are people who feel as if life itself has left them on a doorstep or thrown them away. Abandonment is about loss of love itself, that crucial loss of feeling a connection. It often involves breakup, betrayal and feelings of loneliness — something people can experience all at once, or over a period of months and sometimes even years later as an aftershock. Abandonment means different things to different people. It is an extremely personal and individual experience. Sometimes it is a lingering grief caused by old losses. Sometimes it is fear. Sometimes it can be an invisible barrier holding us back from forming relationships, from reaching our true potential. It can take the form of self-sabotage. We get caught up in patterns of abandonment.

This book provides real help for those who have searched but found nothing to ease the pain of abandonment, and for the ones who want to hasten the speed of recovery. It guides you through what I've observed in years of practice through five universal stages of abandonment. As you continue along this journey, you will perhaps be surprised to discover that the pain you feel when a loved one has left is not an end but the beginning of a time of personal growth. I may refer to a breakup but the effects of abandonment apply to all types of loss and disconnection, whether it's the loss of a job, a dream, or a friend. It may be a loss of one's home, health, or sense of purpose.

Abandonment is a psychobiological process. I'll share with you recent findings from the field of brain science that shed new light on the biological and chemical processes that underlie our emotional response to loss and the most effective path to restoring our emotional balance. People going through the anguish of love loss often feel that their lives have been permanently altered, that they will never be the same and that they will never love again. I'm writing to assure you that as devastated as you may be right now, your feelings of despair and hopelessness are in fact temporary, and they are a normal part of grieving over a relationship. In fact, only by grappling with the feeling that your life is over can you cleanse your deepest wounds from past and present losses and build youself anew. Those of you who have been left to pick up the pieces may wonder about your lost partners, who have already replaced you with new lives and new relationships, while you've been left to do the soul-searching.

You are a part of the chosen group able to undertake this journey. As you continue with the book, you will discover that the pain you are feeling is real, it is part of life, and it is necessary. Anyone who feels this pain is in a legitimate emotional crisis. Many feel as if they have been stabbed in the heart so many times that they don't know which hole to plug in first. But these overwhelming feelings do not in any way imply that you are weak, dependent or undeserving. In spite of the intensity of your feelings, you are still the competent, responsible person you thought you were. Your breakup, with all of its emotional excess, has not diminished you. In fact, being able to feel so deeply is a testament to your strength and tenacity. People are stronger when they are broken. Only by listening to your feelings can you find your way out of them.

This is a time of personal reckoning, but this soul-searching can also lead to extreme self-doubt and self-recrimination. When someone we love rejects us we often turn the anger we feel toward that person against ourselves and blame ourselves for the loss. In this way, abandonment acts like quicksands, pointing us towards feelings of worthlessness and despair. No matter how hurtful or demoralizing the circumstances may have been, you are not a victim or undeserving of love. The fact that someone has chosen not to be with you says as much about your ex as it does about you and how well you functioned in the relationship. You may be humbled for the moment, but you have not been vanquished. Facing these issues and putting what you have experienced into perspective prevents you from turning your anger inward. As you learn to resist the gravitational pull on your self-esteem, you gain strength and emotional endurance. Rather than feeling defeated by your experience, you emerge from it wiser, more self-reliant, and more capable of love. Without guidance, many people don't completely recover from the loss of love. Their fears and doubts remain unresolved. True recovery means confronting uncomfortable feelings, understanding what they are, and, most importantly, learning how to deal with them.

There are some feelings no one wants to talk about because they involve fear, despair, and self-doubt so intense that you're naturally humiliated and ashamed by them. This shame is not just about the embarrassment you may feel over having been rejected; it is about feelings that bewilder you with their potency, induce panic, and have you believing you are weak, dependent, unlovable, even repulsive. Until these intense feelings are addressed, people tend to suffer in silence or try to deny them. Eventually, these forgotten, deeply buried feelings are transformed into an elusive grief. Many seek therapy for this grief but can't seem to overcome that undifferentiated emptiness so often misdiagnosed and treated as depression. (For some people, this persistent grief can involve chemical imbalances that, in some cases, do respond to medication.)

Abandonment is a complex issue, and its wounds can be deeply entrenched. It is important to realize that your feelings, no matter how intense, do not signify a lack of will or frailty of character. They are normal and part of a process that leads to renewal and change. The healing process I'll describe doesn't limit itself to your current loss. It gets to the heart of your cumulative wound—the one that contains all of your disappointments and heartbreaks that have been bubbling beneath the surface of your life, perhaps since childhood. Unresolved abandonment may be the underlying issue responsible for most of the ailments you have been struggling with all along: the insecurity that plagues your relationships, depression and anxiety, obsessive and compulsive behaviors, low energy levels and the loss of self-esteem that have been holding you back. Yet often, people who have been abandoned can't name what they are going through. They may have grown up with an alcoholic parent or felt excluded from their peer group at crucial moments, just as their sense of self was beginning to develop. However detached they may be from the root of their distress, they spend their life energy bargaining with fear and fighting insecurity.

Having lost touch with the source of their wounds, many resort to quick fixes and gratify themselves with food, alcohol, shopping, or other people. They might become addicted to self-help lectures, books and tapes. But all of the self-medicating and soothing words in the world will not erase their distress. In order to do that, you must embark upon a journey that addresses the underlying cause—the abandonment wound itself. This is a journey from which all people can benefit. Through my own experience and through my years of work with others, I have seen how helpful it is to come out of isolation and commune with others as we learn about the grief process that has gripped our lives. For this reason, in addition to running abandonment recovery workshops, I developed an easy format and help to set up ongoing abandonment support groups throughout the country so that you can join together in your local communities and enhance one another's recovery. (See my note section for information.) Wherever you are in the five stages this book describes, you are not alone. It is a revelation to discover that the pain debilitates the strongest, smartest, most self-sufficient among us; that it cuts across all ages, cultures, and status levels; and that it ultimately is a universal human experience. This book is designed to serve as your companion and guide, addressing your most difficult feelings, validating your experience with research from related scientific fields, and giving you the tools you'll need on your journey towards a new outlook and new love.

What Is Abandonment?

- ✓ A feeling
- ✓ A feeling of isolation within a relationship
- ✓ An intense feeling of devastation when a relationship ends
- ✓ A primal fear—the raw element that makes going through heartbreak, divorce, separation, or bereavement cut so deep
- ✓ An aloneness not by choice
- ✓ An experience from childhood
- ✓ A baby left on the doorstep
- ✓ A divorce
- ✓ A woman left by her husband of twenty years for another woman
- ✓ A man being left by his fiancée for someone "more successful"
- ✓ A mother leaving her children

- ✓ A father leaving his children
- ✓ A friend feeling deserted by a friend
- ✓ A child whose pet dies
- ✓ A little girl grieving over the death of her mother
- ✓ A little boy wanting his mommy to come pick him up from nursery school
- ✓ A child who feels replaced by the birth of another sibling
- ✓ A child feeling restless because of his parent's emotional unavailability
- ✓ A boy realizing that he is gay and anticipating the reaction of his parents and friends
- ✓ A teenager feeling that her heart is actually broken
- ✓ A teenage boy afraid to approach the girl he loves
- ✓ A woman who has raised now-grown children feeling empty, as if she has been deserted
- ✓ A child stricken with a serious illness watching his friends play while he must use a wheelchair or remain in bed
- ✓ A woman who has lost her job and with it her professional identity, financial security, and status
- ✓ A man who has been put out to pasture by his company, as if he is obsolete
- ✓ A dying woman who fears being abandoned by loved ones as much as or more than she fears pain and death

Abandonment is all of this and more. Its wound is at the heart of human experience.

Do you struggle with fear of abandonment? You may be profoundly aware of it or you may have a nagging feeling that it's impacting your relationships and your life. Let's look at some of the ways in which fear of abandonment can create a barrier to lasting and loving relationships. ... Do you feel like you have to be perfect or you will be rejected? Do you tolerate criticism or other emotional abuse to avoid being alone? Do you hide your true self because you feel that you will be found not good enough? Do you panic when you don't receive an immediate response to a text, email, or voicemail? Do you become clingy or demanding when you feel someone pulling away? Or do you leave before you can be left? Do you try to avoid your profound fear of abandonment by focusing on work or numbing out with food, alcohol or drugs? Do others' explained or unexplained absences send you into a tailspin? Do you stay in unhealthy relationships because it's better than being alone? Or do you avoid relationships because you fear the ultimate outcome— you will be left?

These thoughts and fears can trigger powerful and painful emotions—shame, sadness, loneliness, longing, anger, and anxiety. These emotions can feel intolerable, and the desire to get rid of them or minimize them can cause you to behave in ways that may have worked in the past. Now, as you assess the relationships in your life, you may have the realization that your behaviors aren't working anymore. You know this because you don't have the relationship that you want. At the same time, the goal of having a healthy, lasting, and loving relationship may feel out of reach to you, or you may feel that it's going to require too much work and you don't have the time or energy. I understand. It's normal to feel that it's easier to lower expectations and hope rather than increase drive and determination, especially in matters of the heart where we have a constant fear of being hurt or disappointed. You may be asking yourself if it's worth it to risk making yourself vulnerable to the possibility of more emotional pain when you feel like you've experienced enough for a lifetime. We all know the pain of being in a relationship that leaves us feeling sad, lonely, misunderstood, unlovable, unsafe, and longing for more (but not necessarily believing that we deserve more). Many of us don't know what it's like to be in a healthy relationship that makes us feel loved, worthy, understood, valued, respected and appreciated for who we are—flaws and all.

What if you could put your fears—and your beliefs about yourself, others, and your relationships—in a new context that would get you distance from your past and allow you to build lasting and loving relationships? What if you could learn new ways to deal with painful emotions and negative thoughts? What if you could make behavioral choices that would get you closer to having that healthy relationship that you long for (but fear you might never have)?

CHAPTER 1

CHANGING COURSE

"I don't know when my parents began their war against each other, but I do know the only prisoners they took were their children. When we needed to escape, we developed a ritual—we found a silent soothing world where there was no pain, a world without mothers and fathers. But that was a long time ago, before I chose not to have a memory." —Pat Conroy, The Prince of Tides

"Forgiving is not forgetting. It is remembering and letting go." —Claudia Black

"I've spent my whole life trying to take the pain out of everyone else's life! The whole time, the issue was my pain, not theirs. Today I don't run scared. I know my fear, my hurt, my anger. I also know my joy. Today I don't live in shame." —Lynn

"Fear and loneliness were all I ever knew—I think I came into this world scared. But now, at forty-two it's different. I have used most things— gambling, women, sex, alcohol—to medicate my fears and not feel so lonely. Today I no longer use people, activities, and substances to medicate or keep me separated from my feelings. I've slowed down to be able to meet myself. And I realize I am okay. I am more than okay! I actually look forward to each day." —Joe

"I wanted so badly to be loved, but for years all I felt was ignored and unwanted. I went to every length possible to make people love me, only to be repeatedly ignored and unwanted. Then, slowly, with the understanding of what had happened in my life and with the freedom to talk about it, things started to turn around. I learned to love myself. What a revelation!" —Judy

These people endured decades of pain and then discovered a different way of being in this world, a different way of living their lives. Why did they have pain? How did it go away? What was their turning point? How did they change the course of their lives? These are some of the questions we will try to answer here.

When we grow up with fear and shame we become adults who live with fear and shame. Accompanying these intense feelings is a pervasive, chronic sense of loss, ranging anywhere from serious to profound. The sensation of this loss goes by various names: unhappiness, hopelessness, depression, emptiness, insecurity, anxiety, boredom. Whatever the words we use, these wounds have troubled our very spirit. We need to let go of the fear and shame. We need to change our course by putting the cause of our pain in its proper perspective. What you might be feeling depends on what you felt when the original wounding began, compounded by your life experiences from that time on. It will be difficult to look back at those troubling times, but this is where your recovery begins.

For some of us, life in our early years was organized around our mother's drinking, and the subsequent embarrassment and shame. Or our brother's dying and the fear, stigma, and prevailing sadness we endured. Or our father's rigid religious fervor and the shame, confusion, guilt, and anger we felt. Or our parents' outright abandonment of their parenting roles and the ensuing abandonment of us, their children. Or our physical or sexual abuse by someone who was supposed to love us.

Early on, we were deprived of the very conditions necessary for us to thrive as children. We lost the opportunity to be ourselves. We lived as characters in someone else's drama, a story of his or her war against pain. The family spotlight was nearly always on that other person, and we were merely bit players, "lesser lights" whose characters were never developed in the family script. The lines we were supposed to speak and our range of emotions were limited so that we didn't conflict with the main character who, in essence, stole the show.

Many others of us accept the idea of chronic loss, but we can't put our finger on any specific event that was the cause of that loss. Perhaps there was no identifiable abuse, addiction, or other blatant dysfunction in our lives. In our case, the loss was growing in the shadow of our parents' pain. Factoring in what we know now, we would probably see that our parents themselves had been character actors in someone else's play. In many ways, the other play is still going on off-stage in the wings of our lives. As a result, what happened in our families was far less obvious, but we were affected nonetheless. Whether we grew up in a subtly or blatantly painful family, we learned to push our concerns aside and stuff our feelings away.

Living by the Rules: Don't Talk, Don't Trust, Don't Feel

"I have this great job. I travel. I'm self-sufficient. Maybe I don't need to be able to get closer to people."

"I'm fifty-two years old. Why should I be angry with my dad for being a victim of his era? All dads hit their kids once in awhile. So my dad made bruises! My life isn't so bad."

"My mother created a lot of pain in my life, being so critical and acting like a jealous girlfriend, but she was also all I had. It could have been worse."

There are always other people who have had greater difficulty, more pain in their lives; the fact that others had it worse doesn't take away your loss. There will always be a greater horror story. Your loss is not negated by someone else's. Your loss is your own pain. How do you go from living according to the rules—Don't Talk, Don't Trust, Don't Feel—to a life where you are free to talk and trust and feel? You do this through a process that teaches you to go to the source of those old, trans-generational rules, to question them and to recreate new rules of your own. You will also have to grieve what is now in the past but is still painful. You will discover that your life will change course as a result of this process of renewal.

Going Back to the Past

"My friends have given me all the books, but I don't want to touch those issues."

"I'm twenty-three. I want to move on in my life. Why all this recovery stuff ?"

"Why would I want to talk about that now? It was a long time ago."

Whenever we explore our past, there's a reason. People who resist going back to face difficult childhood issues are not fully acknowledging the pain of the loss or trauma that occurred in their lives. For many people it has become easier to develop defenses to avoid facing their pain—workaholism, excessiveness in sexual or eating behaviors, perfectionism or extreme caretaking, for instance. These behaviors are often culturally supported. They anesthetize pain and possibly offer esteem. All of this causes people to question why they should want to change. While you can't relive those early years, you can recover from the pain of the past—gradually. Little by little, you can let down those defenses that once helped you survive but are actually hurting you now. No more secret shame. No more need to make a superhuman effort to stay in control so you can keep up appearances. No more need to protect your vulnerability and hide your true self from others. No more need to put up barriers that keep people at a distance.

This new way of living is possible for those who choose it—whenever they choose it. Young, middle-aged, or older, whatever your age, recovery is there if you want it. Recovery starts with recognizing that you would like at least part of your life to be different than it is now.

This book offers a framework for understanding the recovery/healing process from childhood family pain that has carried forward in your life. The book will help you to understand the beliefs and behaviors that have perpetuated your pain. It will identify specific steps in recovery, examine the core issues you will face, and offer guidelines regarding expectations for yourself and others you care about. All of our lives can be viewed on a continuum from "No Pain" to "All Pain," and the combined effect of our experiences, past and present, falls somewhere between these extremes. There is no amount you must have suffered in order to have permission to heal.

Yet, for children raised in troubled families, these basic rights are lost. Instead, they must struggle for the right merely to survive. As a consequence of their loss, these adult-age individuals have difficulty experiencing a healthy life until the child within each of them is able to speak the truth about childhood and get free from the bondage of the past. Until this recognition and healing occurs, people are subject to live a life without choice, reliving old pain and controlling the pain in hurtful ways. Unless something changes, they are characters trapped in their old life dramas, destined to live out old scripts.

Reflect on the statement, "At birth a child has a bill of rights." How strongly do you agree or disagree with this statement?

Chronic Loss and Abandonment

A family's life together is troubled when the conditions that foster physical and emotional growth and well-being are continuously absent over time. The absence of these nurturing conditions has the cumulative effect of creating a childhood experience of chronic loss and abandonment. Within a family, the dynamics that create a sense of loss are denial, rigidity, isolation, and shame. Everyone will experience these things occasionally, but when children experience any of these four factors to a severe degree they carry forward an overriding sense of chronic loss.

Some Loss Is Necessary; Some Is Not

We all experience loss in life. From birth we embark on a journey of separation from our fathers and mothers. The losses we experience are natural or "necessary losses" and are balanced by gains that build our strength and health. Children naturally experience loss of some level of security as they enter school. There is a sense of loss when children move to a new area and a new home. They experience another kind of natural loss through the death of a loved one, whether it is a family member, friend, or pet.

A common natural loss is that of a pet. This is a painful time and often a child's first experience with death. As painful as that can be, it is less so in our father's or mother's arms. In a troubled family, children are often not supported in their pain or are told not to show what they feel. Sometimes they're also told not to feel what they feel—to keep a stiff upper lip, to stop crying—to stop acting like a child. In a severely dysfunctional family, the scenario might be that one parent intentionally causes the loss—for example, by giving away the child's cat—and the other parent denies the significance of what happened, maybe even denies that it happened at all. When we experience a natural loss and are supported by our parents we feel sad, but loved and secure. When we are not supported we feel sad, unloved, abandoned. This lack of support or help with our pain is, then, an abandonment experience.

Abandonment Is Not a Necessary Loss

"Oh sure, I remember the first day of school. Don't we all? My seven-year old sister woke me up yelling. She dressed me while Mom was sleeping. Dad was away. She held my hand, took me to her school, and told me to stay away from the older kids and not to fall asleep."

"Two different times growing up my father actually gave our dogs away—our pets! My best friends! My parents told us both times that they were killed by cars, but I overheard Mom telling Grandma the real story!"

"I remember my graduation. My dad was too busy to get there until it was over."

These are examples of children who were emotionally abandoned. They were not offered solace, direction, or support at significant times in their lives. Many of us are not offered protection at times of natural loss; we may even be in families that create losses for children. What is most damaging is that these losses take place at the time in life when we are developing our self-worth.

The losses are most often due to emotional abandonment, physical abandonment, or a combination of the two.

Emotional abandonment occurs when the parent or primary caretaker is not emotionally available to the child on a consistent basis. While physical needs are being met, there is little or no nurturing, hugging, or emotional intimacy developing between the parent and the child. The unnecessary losses a child experiences may range from loss of quality and quantity of time with a parent, loss of childhood as a result of unrealistic expectations placed on the child, loss of hope, loss of opportunity, to loss of innocence.

"By the time I was seven, I was the little adult at home. I had to be perfect. There was no laughter, no fun, no tenderness."

"After my third foster home, I knew no one was coming for me."

"My dad didn't care about me. He clearly liked being away from home better than he liked us kids. By the time I was eleven, I didn't care much about things either. No one had time for me, so what did it matter if I was a screw up?"

Loss is not always a result of what does happen; sometimes loss is the result of what does not happen. Maybe you had a need that went unnoticed.

Maybe you did not hear a parent say, "I love you" or "You are special." The loss could also be a result of what you didn't get to say because your parents weren't available, or what you didn't get to do with them, such as play or work on projects. Words and time are important to all children as they grow up. They convey to us that we are valued. Physical abandonment occurs when a child has repetitively missed meals, has been left alone for hours or days unsupervised, or has been left without adequate supervision. Due to our ability to deny, we sometimes negate our abandonment. "I was always supervised. Maybe Mom and Dad weren't home, but my older brother was." Although being left with older siblings for lengthy periods of time may illustrate one child's valiant effort to protect another child, it still constitutes abandonment by parents. In spite of the maturity of our nine-, twelve-, or fifteen-year-old siblings, they are still nine, twelve, or fifteen. We needed adult supervision and protection. Not being properly clothed or not having physical protection are forms of abandonment.

Physical and sexual abuse are major boundary violations. It is an act of physical abandonment when the child is treated as an object and not as a person. Those who are responsible for you owe it to you to see that you are not violated. You deserve protection. Not feeling secure, protected, safe, both psychologically and physically, creates the greatest loss for children. The messages heard by the child experiencing emotional abandonment and physical abandonment are very similar: "You are not of value, you are not wanted, you are in the way."

Being in a family where there is chronic loss is traumatic; it gravely interferes with our ability to feel good about ourselves and the world. It can interfere with developing skills that lead to connecting and bonding. It will be significant in the creation of internalized fear and shame.

Denial

Denial is a defense mechanism, a natural response to protect against pain. When someone feels helpless to impact their situation or is ashamed of what is occurring, they often resort to denial. Denial can be identified when individuals discount, minimize, or rationalize their feelings. As a nine-year-old put it, "Denial is pretending things are different than how they really are." While the word denial is most often associated with the addictive family, it is the central dynamic of any dysfunctional system. To be raised with denial is to know the Rule of Silence. As children we learned that it was not okay to speak our truth and, instead, we should pretend things were different than they were. It may be that our perceptions were not validated, or we felt threatened about speaking up for fear of the consequences or punishment. We may have felt hopeless, believing that nothing good would come from talking. As children raised with the Rule of Silence we became confused about loyalty. Often we didn't speak up because we were afraid we wouldn't be believed. As upset, frightened, or concerned as we were, we believed that we would jeopardize our well-being and betray those we loved if we spoke our truth.

If we were raised with others close to us also subscribing to the Rule of Silence, we had no practice trusting that those we spoke to would hear us.

Many of us just didn't know what to say. We couldn't make sense of people's behavior. We didn't understand or know what was really happening and we had no language to describe it. What we knew most were our feelings and it was made clear to us that we weren't supposed to talk about them. Growing up with denial makes it easy to be in denial today—and not know it. We discount our feelings and perceptions. We rationalize hurtful behaviors. Today, we may say we aren't angry, disappointed, or hurt when we are. We tell ourselves something isn't important when it is. We even tell ourselves certain things don't happen much when they occur frequently. We don't speak our truth. When we spend years learning to minimize, discount, or rationalize, it's only normal to continue to do so as adults. We are so skilled in denying that we do it without conscious thought. Consider reflecting on the family in which you were raised and make a list of the things you could easily talk about. Make a list of those subjects it was not okay to talk openly about.

Rigidity

In troubled families parents are often dogmatic in their thinking: "Things will be this way and there are no exceptions." The old adage, "Children are to be seen and not heard" is often adhered to. Inherent in this stance are the Don't Question and Don't Think rules. This is a family where it is never okay to challenge authority and under the guise of respect you are to quietly submit. Often, the rigidity is evident in the structure that is imposed on the children. There may be a lack of fairness regarding family rules and expectations. Parents are unrealistic, expecting far too much from their children. They aren't age appropriate in their expectations, such as expecting a six year- old to do what is normal for a twelve-year-old. While children need consistency, rigid controls are discouraging and debilitating. "We weren't allowed out of the house outside of school and church. We couldn't have friends in. We always had chores or had to be doing schoolwork even when there was none to do."

Not only is this rigidity often isolating for a child, but typically there are no rewards for the child who obeys. There is little likelihood the child is ever celebrated. To obey is an expectation; to perform is a requirement.

In time the child finds no joy, feels the pain of isolation, and ultimately, if the child does not succumb to depression, the child will find hurtful ways in which to act out. As a consequence of growing up with rigidity, we as adults are often rigid in our thinking. We have difficulty perceiving choices. We are unrealistic with ourselves and others, setting ourselves or others up to "never be good enough. "We cannot find joy in our accomplishments. Or, we rebel and take on a permissive attitude with ourselves, often resulting in difficulty with being accountable and responsible. If you identify with being raised in a rigid family system, describe the impact it has had on you.

Isolation

Emotional isolation is also a common experience for children in troubled families. Isolation is particularly damaging because we need a connection with others to create meaning in life. Yet we live life as if in a bubble, shouting, "Hello out there—I'm alive in here! Does anybody hear me?" But no one answers.

We have learned to live with emotional isolation as a result of not being able to speak the truth. Shelley, age thirteen, depicts the isolation we know so well. When asked to draw a picture of her home, she showed her bedroom and the living room amplified in size. In the living room the parents were portrayed as being in a heated argument; there were footprints running from the living room to a bedroom where you then saw Shelley and her two sisters hiding at opposite ends of the room from each other behind separate beds. Even in crisis the sisters were unable to connect, to bond, to be of support to each other.

The emotional isolation within the home often carries over to those outside of the family as well. We don't want others to know of our personal pain or the family pain. We are afraid of how others would respond if they knew. As adults we have come to be socially isolated, or we surround ourselves with others while withholding our true feelings and thoughts. The family rules, Don't Talk, Don't Trust, Don't Feel, create our isolation. While we may have social graces, our hallmark is superficiality. Draw a picture of the family in which you were raised that represents the closeness or lack of closeness you felt with the different family members.

Shame

Internalized shame becomes the foundation of a person's trauma. Shame is the painful feeling that comes with the belief there is something inherently wrong with who you are. It is the belief that you, or a part of you, is defective or inadequate. Words that describe shame are reflective of seeing oneself as "bad," "ugly," "stupid," "incompetent," "damaged." To live with shame is to feel alienated and defeated, never quite good enough to belong. It is an isolating experience that makes us think we are completely alone and unique in our belief that we are unlovable. Secretly, we feel like we are to blame. Any and all deficiency lies within ourselves. Gershen Kaufman, author of Shame: The Power of Caring, said that "shame is without parallel, a sickness of the soul." Shame reflects an internal darkness in one's soul. And it is because of this our recovery truly has spiritual meaning.

Underneath layers of shame you will find that abandonment is at the foundation. Abandonment, as described earlier, may be emotional or physical. But abandonment is most often experienced through various forms of rejection, rejection that has been colored by parental words and actions, some subtle, some not so subtle. It is useful to visualize a continuum, with acceptance at one end, rejection at the other end, and many shades of emotional unavailability or parental indifference to your needs and wants somewhere between.

No one's family is perfect; parents are people who, like everyone else, have weaknesses and faults; they often make mistakes. But anyone who has lived with chronic loss—loss resulting from a mixture of rigidity, denial, isolation, and shame—deserves the opportunity to heal.

The Impact of Our Losses

It is not possible to live with the dynamics of chronic loss and not be affected. While families have many common characteristics, there are all kinds of experiences that create differences. Some of these experiences impact us more negatively than others. There are many variables that create differences in the ways and the depth we feel the effects.

- Age at onset of trauma or loss. The younger we are, the more hurtful it is to us.

- Stigma associated to dynamics. If negative judgments are attached to our experiences, there are greater emotional consequences; i.e., there is greater stigma being in an abusive family than a home characterized by workaholism.

- Connection to outside support system. Connection to extended family, friend's family, extracurricular school activities, the ability to find meaningful relationships and/or activities outside of family lessens our shame.

- Multiple trauma/shame-related dynamics. For example, to live with both addiction and abuse is more traumatic than to live with just one source of pain.

Usually about this stage in reading there is a tendency to begin saying to yourself, "yes, but . . ." ; "yes, but my dad wasn't all bad, he did do some good

things in his parenting"; or "yes, but my mother did teach me . . ." In spite of any loss or pain in one's growing up years, we were given gifts by our parents. Those gifts will be ours to cherish. There is no doubt that we come from families with a matrix of strengths and vulnerabilities. It is also clear that the survival skills one developed helped to create important personal strengths. To bring about greater predictability in our young lives and defend against the pain, we developed ways of coping that may have brought a resourcefulness to our personalities. Yet we need to be cautious that we do not reinstate the Don't Talk or Don't Question rules by discounting the pain, all for the sake of recognizing how strong we are. Please recognize that owning the pain that occurred in our lives in no manner lessens the gifts we were given and the strengths we have developed.

It is important to identify your losses. Until losses and pain are dealt with directly, the resulting feelings, while often masked, are carried into adulthood. Unless we have a chance to learn healthy coping skills, this combination of past loss and pain leads to severe consequences creating even more pain in the present.

Changing Course

To change course, be it a minor shift or a major turn in your life, does not mean giving up who you are—it means letting go of who you are not. It means letting go of your pain. You are not your pain. You will need to walk through the pain. However, you do not have to walk through the pain alone again as a helpless, vulnerable child. Remember, whatever you experienced as a child, your perceptions and interpretations were those of a child. The perceived belief that you were worthless or bad is not true. You never were bad or unworthy, and you are not today. It is my hope that, in time, you will be able to say and to believe in your heart, "I am good. I am adequate. I am worthy."

It means letting go of an undesirable family script. You are no longer an unwitting character in someone else's life now that you understand you have the freedom to choose. Each insight into your past and its connection to your present is like turning on the light in a dark room. It doesn't change what is there, but now that you can see where you are going, you can go in and out freely without harm. Fear no longer drives you—freedom moves you. Each of these awarenesses bring you new choices. Each new awareness is a turning point.

CHAPTER 2

YOU CAN'T GO FORWARD WITHOUT FINISHING THE PAST

"In this dream I was stationed underground, in the grave. . . .This was my company, my life, my mission—to watch over the bones. And then slowly. . . . I walked away and climbed out of the grave, into the sun and the wide expanse of the world. . . . I turned one last time to say good-bye. The vigil was over." —John

"To free yourself from the past you must break the rules of silence and compliance." —Claudia Black

When children are raised with chronic loss, without the psychological or physical protection they need and certainly deserve, it is most natural for them to internalize incredible fear. Not receiving the necessary psychological or physical protection equals abandonment. And, living with repeated abandonment experiences creates shame. Shame arises from the painful message implied in abandonment: "You are not important. You are not of value." Unresolved pain of the past and pain in the present created by past-driven behaviors fuel our fear of abandonment and shame. This is the pain from which we need to heal.

PAIN FROM THE PAST

Physical Abandonment

For some children abandonment is primarily physical. Physical abandonment occurs when the physical conditions necessary for thriving have been replaced by:

- lack of appropriate supervision.
- inadequate provision of nutrition and meals.
- inadequate clothing, housing, heat, or shelter; physical and/or sexual abuse.

As children, we are totally dependent on our caretakers to provide safety in our environment. When they do not, we grow up believing that the world is an unsafe place, that people are not to be trusted, and that we do not deserve positive attention and adequate care.

Emotional Abandonment

Emotional abandonment occurs when parents do not provide the emotional conditions and emotional environment necessary for healthy development. Because more people experience emotional abandonment than physical abandonment, and because it is a more subtle dynamic, the following experiences may be helpful to understanding emotional abandonment. There are two frameworks for abandonment that can simplify the term.

1. Abandonment is experienced by parental indifference to a child's needs and wants, or the parents (or other primary caregivers) are emotionally unavailable on an ongoing basis. They do not offer the support and nurturance a child needs. Therefore the child can neither experience nor express his or her feelings appropriately.

2. Abandonment occurs when a child has to hide a part of who he or she is in order to be accepted (while others do this to avoid rejection), such as when

- it is not proper in your family to make a mistake.

- it is not okay in your family to show feelings, being told the way you feel is not true or okay. "You have nothing to cry about and if you don't stop crying I will really give you something to cry about." "That really didn't hurt." "You have nothing to be angry about." When in fact the child is feeling great fear, sadness, pain, or anger. We are not talking about the occasional time a parent becomes frustrated with a child and makes such a comment, but a family situation where there is continual discounting of a child's emotions.

- it is not okay in your family to have needs. Everyone else's needs appear to be more important than yours, and the only way you even get attention is by attending to the needs of others.

- it is not okay to have successes. Accomplishments are not acknowledged, are many times discounted, or even used as ammunition to shame a child.

- Other acts of abandonment occur when:

- children cannot live up to the expectations of their parents. These expectations are often unrealistic and not age-appropriate, such as expecting the eight-year-old to remember her dental appointment or the twelve-year-old to be able to manage his younger siblings for hours at a time.

- children are held responsible for other people's behavior. They may be consistently blamed for the actions and feelings of their parents.

- disapproval is shown toward children that is aimed at their entire being or identity rather than a particular behavior, such as telling a child he is worthless when he does not do his homework or she is never going to be a good athlete because she missed the final catch of the game. Who the child is, is not separated out from what the child does.

Abandonment and Boundaries

Many times our abandonment issues are fused with distorted, confused, or undefined personal boundaries. We experience abandonment when parents have a distorted sense of boundaries, their boundaries and ours. They want us to like what they like, dress like they dress, and feel as they do. This is particularly painful during our teenage years when, as part of discovering our own self, we seek out behaviors different from our parents'. This teenager/parent struggle is common to many. Some parents cannot recognize this as part of the adolescent stage, but see it as a personal affront to their image and their own sense of worth. If we in any way express differences from our parents, or make different choices than they would, we know we run the risk of rejection. How many of us went to the school of our father's choosing because he had wanted to attend but had been unable to? How many entered into careers that our parents chose for us? How many of us married who we did or when we did because our parents desired it? I offer a caution in that having done what our parents expected, wanted, or demanded does not mean that it was the wrong thing to do. It just so often means that the decision was never totally ours. It is the process that is more painful or possibly wrong, not necessarily the outcome.

Maddy told how her mother spoke as if it were simply fact that neither of her daughters were to have children due to the possibility of transmitting a terminal genetic disease. "My mom made it clear that it was not an option for me. Because that decision seemed based in her wanting to protect us from pain, and to protect a child from a premature death, it was hard to want to question this dictate. Mom's motivation was sincere. But I was twenty-nine years old when I realized I had never made my own decision about this. Until then it had been my mother's dictate. I realized I had to sit down and separate my life choices from my mother's pain in having a child who died young. I wrestled with the decision for a few years and ultimately made the decision to not have a child. Today, the decision is mine, not my mother's."

Certainly, many people do exactly what their parents don't want them to do. Often this is a part of their attempt to be a separate person. We don't marry the person our father liked so much. We don't go to the college our mother aspired to attend. Often we choose to marry the person they would like the least or simply choose to not attend college at all. Again, it is not the outcome that is the issue as much as it is the decision-making process. Instead of choosing freely, we make a reactive decision based in anger.

When parents hold children responsible for what should be their responsibility, such as telling the child it is his or her behavior that has caused the breakup of the parents' marriage, or it is the child's behavior that creates the stress that results in the parent's need to drink or use drugs, they are expecting something impossible of a child. In effect, they are telling children that they have more power than they truly have, setting them up to experience futility and inadequacy. Henri still feels pain when he talks about how his father publicly gloated over Henri's accomplishments. "Some people told me I should be grateful that my dad even noticed what I was involved in. But there was always something missing about his being proud of me. When I was growing up, I did well in school; I was a very good athlete. I was a student leader and often had my picture in the local paper. My dad came to my events, boasting about me in a way that never seemed real. His boasting was so grand and his need for people to know I was his son was so strong. Yet there was this total lack of interest in me when I was home. When I got home from the ball games, he would already be in bed. He never boasted to me. He never once congratulated me or patted me on the back."

What is important to note is that Henri did not get the validation he needed to feel special, important, or of value to his father. What he believed was that his value to his father was in how he could make his father look to his father's peers. Many times parents develop relationships with their children in which they are their friends, their peers, their equals. In doing so, they share information that is not age-appropriate for a child. Inappropriate information often creates a sense of burden, or even guilt, for children; that is not fair. To tell a ten-year-old daughter that her father has had an affair cannot offer the daughter any security. The mother may need to talk about it, but that needs to be with someone who has the adult resources to be able to offer appropriate support or feedback. To share with an eight-year-old son the fears related to a situation at work only makes the child feel that his parent is too vulnerable to be available as a source of protection. When parents are disrespectful of their children's boundaries and violate them, the message given is that they don't value the child as a person. That message becomes internalized as "I am not of value. I am not worthy." When parents don't acknowledge children's boundaries, the message they give is "You are here to meet my needs," "I am more important than you," and/or "It is not okay to be your own person with individual feelings, desires, or needs." The message also implies that the children have to give up themselves to be available to another. This internalizes to the belief, "I am bad for having different or separate needs, wants, and feelings." "I, in my uniqueness, am not of value. "When children experience chronic abandonment with distorted boundaries, they live in fear and doubt about their worth. The greater the clarity a child has around boundaries, understanding who is responsible for what, and the greater a child's self-esteem, the more likely a child will be able to reject, rather than internalize, shameful behaviors and messages.

The following is an example of a young person, Sandi, who, in spite of the fact that she was raised in an alcoholic family, experienced some stability in her early years. As a result, she developed a sense of autonomy and self-esteem, which helped her ward off shame. "Up until I was about eight, home seemed okay. I felt valued, life was fun. Then as if it was overnight, my dad was always angry. My mom was preoccupied and distant or very sad. It was as if neither of our parents had any time for us. Looking back now I realize that something was happening. I just couldn't figure it out. No one was talking about what was wrong. Life just became more and more frightening. I tried to not get in the way. I took care of my brother and sister. I tried to do things to make my dad and mom happy. Nothing I did really made a difference."

One night when she was sixteen and cheerleading at a basketball game, her father showed up so drunk he could hardly walk on his own and created a scene that nearly incited a racial riot. With his arms thrown over her shoulders and her pom-poms tucked under her arms, Sandi was leading her drunk father out of the gym when he began to scream racial slurs at a group of African American teenagers. "He said things I never heard him or anyone else say," Sandi said. "He said things I never knew he thought. Thank heaven this group of kids couldn't reach us. It was all I could do to get him out of the gym. Everyone was screaming and jeering. Well, I got him into his friend's car and off they went. I didn't know why my dad acted like he did—I was so angry at him."

Sandi had the ability to be angry because she had not previously internalized shame and therefore could clearly differentiate who was responsible for what. She had healthy boundary distinction. She knew what took place in the gym was about her father, not her. Because she did not take this incident as a statement about her worth or value, she was also able to access other feelings. With shame we lose the ability to identify our feelings and are more likely to reinstate the Don't Talk rule. Sandi said she was angry, and then became sad. She could talk about her fear. While this scene was certainly an act of abandonment by her father, she nonetheless had an emotional boundary that protected her self-worth and her autonomy.

Sandi's ability to maintain a healthy emotional boundary ("My father's behavior does not determine who I am") prevented her from feeling shamed and personally diminished by her father's behavior.

Linda was born into an already hectic, frightened family. Her first memories were of hiding behind a table in the kitchen, trying not to be noticed, while listening to her parents arguing and thinking to herself, "Just don't let them see me." She spent most of her life trying to be invisible. "In my family there was a lot of arguing, unhappiness, and a lot of moving from place to place. I was the youngest of four and an unplanned pregnancy. My mother let me know right away that she was content with three babies, not four. I felt I came out of the chute needing a protective shield, trying to ward off the hurtful words, the painful glares. I was always in their way, yet I worked so hard not to be. My very existence seemed like such a thorn." When childhood is spent on survival, such as Linda's was, there is little energy left to develop an autonomous or separate sense of self. Linda was chronically abandoned, subject to emotional boundary abuse; as a result she experienced and internalized shame.

When we are abandoned by our caretakers we do not perceive that they were bad people or what they did to us was bad. As children we cannot reject parents, because they are so desperately needed. Instead, we take the burden of being wrong or bad onto ourselves. In doing this, we purge the caretakers of being wrong or hurtful, which reinforces a sense of security. In essence, outer safety is purchased at the price of inner security. This truth bears repeating because it defines the root of our pain. What we must understand now is that our abandonment experiences and boundary violations were in no way indictments of our innate goodness and value. Instead, they revealed the flawed thinking, false beliefs, and impaired behaviors of those who hurt us. Still, the wounds were struck deep in our young hearts and minds, and the very real pain can still be felt today. The causes of our emotional injury need to be understood and accepted so we can heal. Until we do, the pain will stay with us, becoming a driving force in our adult lives. Describe the ways you experienced physical and/or emotional abandonment in your growing up years.

Past-Driven Present Pain

In recovery we seek to change the course in our present lives by healing the pain of our past. As a result of our experiences,

- we adopted false beliefs; that is, "I can't make a mistake or I will be worthless" or "I have to produce to be of value."

- we learned defense skills; that is, to blame others before they blame us.

- we developed cognitive defense mechanisms; that is, to deny, minimize, or rationalize. We developed mechanisms to distract us from our pain; that is, excessive behaviors such as overeating, drinking, or drug use. All of these are strategies for the preservation of ourselves when our self is threatened.

Jan said, "I knew my parents loved me. They provided for me. They came to my school events. They told me they loved me. They would hug me. Yet, they would blatantly reject me if I showed feelings of sadness or anger. There was clearly a Don't Talk rule around being emotional unless the feelings were positive. My shame was for having feelings. So while I knew I was valued in one way, I felt very rejected and abandoned in other ways. There was a lot of loss in my family. My dad lost his job and did not find one for four years. My mother had to be hospitalized for unknown reasons twice when I was between nine and eleven. My sister went to live with my grandmother during those times. And we weren't to talk about any of this. I was angry. I was very frightened. I was sad. I wanted to scream so I could be heard, and yet knew I would not be heard and only banished further."

Jan did what most of us do when feeling abandonment and fear—she did her best to be "lovable" so her family would be there for her. Being lovable would be defined by others. For Jan, it meant discounting her own feelings and needs and putting those of others ahead of hers, which in turn meant disconnecting from her own feelings and needs. Jan learned these defenses and skills as a young girl; now these are the only defenses and skills she knows for protecting herself and relating to others. Paradoxically, in adulthood, Jan's beliefs and behaviors no longer protect her, but actually cause her more pain. Unfortunately, this pattern will continue throughout her adult life until the painful weight of chronically discounting her needs and feelings is so great that she is no longer able to continue as she has. Then she will seek new, often harmful protectors, such as alcohol, prescription pills, or food. These present-day defenses will only perpetuate, and probably escalate, her pain until she turns from the course of protection to the path of healing.

Most people develop protective strategies when they are young, carrying them into adulthood, often generalizing the impact into other areas of life. For example, as a child you may have used food to medicate your pain, and continue to use food this way as an adult, but now you have also added alcohol as a medication. Or, as a child, if you used people-pleasing behaviors to get attention from parents, you may also employ this strategy to get attention in the workplace; it may also fuel an addictive relationship pattern. The mechanisms we develop to reduce our anxiety and fears are defensive protectors. In no way should we ever be critical of what we needed to do to protect ourselves while growing up. Today, we need to recognize when these defenses and protectors are intrusive in our lives or when they create harm and pain. The purpose or theme of these strategies has been to lessen the pain of abandonment; also to compartmentalize or distance ourselves from the incredible fear and sense of powerlessness. The basis for all these attempts is to control or compensate for the pain.

The burden of pain we presently carry and try so hard to control is the combination of unresolved pain from the past plus pain from the present. As we know, events and family conditions that caused our past pain cannot be changed. Our response to pain is a choice we are making in the present. How we choose to respond can change the course of our lives. In the next few pages, we'll discuss how people respond to pain so we will be able to understand the choices we can make.

Attempts to Control Our Pain

Whether or not we understood the source of our pain in our early lives, we felt it. We were anxious, fearful, saddened, or angry. To live with a high degree of emotional pain was so unbearable for most of us that we sought ways to control the pain to defend against it. Ironically and unfortunately, as we have now seen, those ways of compensating created their own pain. As adults still trying to control our pain, we have sought ways to create a sense of control or power to compensate for the overwhelming experience of powerlessness. We have attempted to control the pain and/or to control the sources of pain. We have tried to be in control to protect ourselves from further exposure so that our vulnerability would not be visible. We have tried to be in control so that no one would ever shame us again and so that we would not have to feel our pain. We feel our pain. We medicate our pain. We rationalize our pain. These are all responses to the pain we have felt for so long. We first respond to pain on an emotional level, most commonly in terms of victimization, rage, and depression. Then, in an attempt to control the pain, we may respond with behaviors that try to medicate it such as alcohol, food and drug abuse, or compulsive behaviors related to sex, money, or relationships. Last, we may respond on a rational level, thinking we can avoid the pain if we don't do anything to cause it. Perfectionism and procrastination are two cognitive attempts to control pain by avoiding it.

EMOTIONAL RESPONSES TO PAIN

Victimization as a Response to Pain

Chronic victimization is the result of when we accept and operate on the shameful messages that we internalized as a result of the abandonment. It is a combination of not believing in our own worth and not developing the skills that go with a belief in our worthiness. Setting limits is one such skill. When we have internalized beliefs, such as "I am not worthy," "I am not of value," "Other people are more important than me," or "Other people are more worthy," then it is difficult to set limits. We don't believe we have the right to set limits. We do not know how to say no. Those of us who are victims struggle with appropriate boundaries. We are most apt not to have boundaries or to have boundaries that are easily permeable. Victims have learned not to trust their own perceptions, believing that another person's perception is more accurate than their own. They always give others the benefit of the doubt and are willing to respond to the structure others set. Victims are not apt to question. In addition to the family rules Don't Talk, Don't Feel, Don't Trust, they have learned the rules Don't Question and Don't Think.

Not believing in their own worth, victims often fail to realize they even have needs and, as a result, do not take care of themselves. They operate from a position of fear, unable to access any anger or indignation that comes with being hurt, disappointed, or even abused. When asked what they need or want, victims often literally do not know. While the development of the victim response is the result of the belief in personal powerlessness, it is clearly a response to the intense emotional pain in one's life. It not only is an outcome of helplessness, it is also a kind of defense in that victims believe they may not have as much pain if they give in and relinquish their autonomy to someone else. Victims have developed a high tolerance for pain and for inappropriate behavior. They have become emotionally separated from themselves by becoming highly skilled at rationalizing, minimizing, and often flatly denying the events and emotions in their lives. They are not as readily able to identify others' behavior that has hurt them because that would, in their perception, create a greater feeling of helplessness or invite more trouble.

Some victims stay in isolation. Those who choose to stay more visible often play a victim/martyr situation: "Look at how I am victimized. Aren't they terrible for doing this to me! I will just have to endure." Being the victim becomes part of a cycle. Victims already feel bad about themselves as a result of being abandoned and/or used and abused. They don't act in a way that provides safety and security for themselves, leading to greater abandonment or abuse. Typically, the greater a person's shame, the more likely he or she will invite someone else with shame into their lives. Very often, for the victim, this other person is someone who appears to have the ability to take charge, make things happen, someone who feels strengthened by association with the victim's vulnerability. Depending on the specific history of the two people involved, that attraction often leads to the dominant one battering the victim, either emotionally or physically.

Almost inevitably, victims have great difficulty protecting themselves in the context of intimate relationships. For example, a woman may have such a desperate longing for nurturance and care that it makes it difficult for her to establish safe and appropriate boundaries with others. Her tendency to denigrate herself and to idealize those to whom she becomes attached further clouds her judgment. Typically, her empathic attunement to the wishes of others and her automatic, often unconscious habits of obedience also tend to make her vulnerable to anyone in a position of power or authority. Her defensive style makes it difficult for her to form conscious and accurate assessments of danger. For all of the reasons noted above, whether male or female, the shameful person is at great risk of repeated victimization.

Rage as Response to Pain

Rage is the holding tank for accumulated fears, angers, humiliations, and shame. It is for many a response of no longer wanting to endure the pain. Emotionally, rage is an attempt to be heard, seen, and valued when people are most desperate and lacking in other resources. For some people rage becomes an integral part of their lifestyle. Growing up, they found anger to be the one safe feeling for them to express, so all their other vulnerabilities were masked with anger. Many people who are rageful don't show any sign of emotions; they keep a tight lid on all of their feelings until something triggers an eruption. There may not be signs of any feeling, and suddenly their rage is in someone else's face. Perhaps it is a scathing memo at work or an outburst of criticism toward a waiter or gas station attendant. It could be a lack of tolerance for any disagreement in a discussion, followed by a theatrical exit, or it may take the form of physical or verbal abuse. People with chronic rage do exist but they are not tolerated in most neighborhoods or communities. They usually live in isolation, often with someone who is the chronic victim of their rage; or they move around a lot, wearing out their welcome after relatively short periods of time in one place.

While we may view others' rage as being out of control, those who are ragers feel very much in control and powerful. In their rage they no longer feel inadequate and defective. Rage is intended to protect against further experiences of pain. Rage is a way of actively compensating for powerlessness and feelings of shame by offering a false but attractive (to the rager) sense of power. When rage is the only way people know to protect against their emptiness, powerlessness, and pain, their choice is a quick one. Rageful behavior also offers protection by keeping people at a distance. As a result, other people cannot see into the raging person's inner self that he or she believes to be so ugly. Rage as a defense also offers protection by transferring the shame to others. The outwardly rageful person chooses a victim-like person who, consciously or not, is willing to take the abuse and take on or assume the shame.

Rage can be accumulated anger that has never seemed safe to expose. When anger is held back, it becomes internalized. With time it grows, festering into chronic bitterness or, even more likely, chronic depression. When there has been no outlet for rage, it is more apt to explode suddenly as a significant single hostile act such as physical abuse or even murder. Such an act is the consequence of the accumulation of feelings combined with the inability to tolerate painful feelings, to resolve conflict, or to perceive options and choices.

Depression as a Response to Pain

Unfortunately, a depressed person is typically pictured as one who sleeps excessively, is unable to eat, and is suicidal. While that picture represents the severe end of the depression continuum, many depressed adults are able to function daily and meet most of their responsibilities. After all, that has been their survival mode. They present a false self to the world that may not have the look of depression, but their true self, their emotional and spiritual self, is experiencing great despair. When this is practiced day in and out, week after week, month after month, and year after year, it can easily translate to being "closeted depressed." To keep depression hidden, those of us who are depressed avoid getting close enough or spending enough time around others who may recognize our true feelings and the pervasive emptiness our depression is masking. We don't develop close friendships where others are invested enough to "pull our covers. "We appear very capable and seem to put out an impenetrable force field that says, "Don't ask me about myself. Don't push me." It is difficult enough being depressed. It is even more difficult when we have shame around it—shame as one cause of depression and added shame because we are depressed.

There are many different theories about the cause of depression. Some clinicians and researchers believe it to be a biochemical imbalance, a disordered neurochemistry, best treated with antidepressants. It is commonly accepted among professionals that depression tends to run in families, suggesting there may be a physiological predisposition toward depression. Other theories support the belief that depression is a consequence of a habitually pessimistic and disordered way of viewing the world. It can also be a consequence of loss and the inability to do the grief work necessary to bring completion to the feelings of sorrow. (Note: A qualified physician needs to assess all depression.) There is tremendous loss associated with being raised in a shame-based family. With the family being denial-centered, as it often is, and it not being okay to talk honestly, the sense of loss is amplified because there is no way to work through the pain. The hurt, the disappointment, the fears, and the angers associated with life events, as well as with abandonment experiences, are all swirled together and internalized. When you add to this a personal belief that says you are at fault, it is easy to see why you came to believe in your unworthiness, and so try to hide your real self from others.

Eventually, whether you are thirty-five or fifty-five, you suddenly hit a wall. The burden of hiding eventually becomes too heavy and all of those protecting, controlling mechanisms that kept you going for so long just stop working. Depression sets in. Most people who experience depression related to loss are extremely frightened of their feelings. And they have so much to feel about. When it is not safe to speak these feelings, they become directed inward against the self. This becomes another means of perpetuating shame, which then further protracts the depressive mood.

As discussed in chapter 1, there are necessary and unnecessary losses in life. Because it was not safe to acknowledge them, we didn't learn coping skills for the losses that would occur in our adult years. So, when a loss occurs and/or accumulates in adulthood, we resort to the same defenses we learned in childhood to deny what we are feeling. When we have had chronic loss in our lives, many of us develop thought processes wherein we catastrophize and exaggerate fear to such a point that we feel hopeless and in despair. For example, when your husband is twenty minutes late for an important appointment, you think he must have been in a terrible car accident. When your boss forgot to say hello, you feel certain that she is angry with you and is going to let you go. Armed with some small bit of knowledge, we presume the worst will happen. Over the years, given our experiences, we have developed a committee of internal voices that have become our Inner Critic, telling ourselves we are stupid, not wanted, ugly, and unimportant; this is in response to any slight or perceived loss, or when we feel slighted by someone we value.

Most adults from troubled families experience a combination of both unresolved loss and a pessimistic view of life. When we feel our powerlessness, our despair, and our fear, we send ourselves into a downhill spiral so quickly anybody's head would be spinning.

Acute Episodes of Depression

Many adults make their way through life cut off from their internal pain, until they experience a significant present-day loss—the last child leaving home, a significant health problem, the death of a close friend or family member, the loss of job or career opportunity. As great numbers of women enter peri-menopausal and menopausal stages, the combination of physical changes and the symbolism around such changes can create an incredible sense of loss. For men and women both, one significant present-day loss can be the straw that breaks the camel's back. In other words, the new loss can trigger the beginning of a downward emotional spiral in which the adult becomes overwhelmed in despair, shame, powerlessness, and depression.

Carmella, who was raised in a physically abusive family, was a department manager in an engineering firm. She had tucked away the pain of her childhood history into a corner of her heart and put a lock on it. She was involved in raising her own family, and kept a distant relationship with her sister and parents. All aspects of her life were compartmentalized. Then one day, she lost her oldest daughter in an accident. Six months after that, her father died. Three weeks later, Carmella made her first suicide attempt. To lose a child is one of life's greatest tragedies for anybody. Further, Carmella had no skills, no internal supports to deal with the intense pain when her daughter died. While she did not feel close to her father, his death unleashed all of the childhood pain she had so neatly and quietly tucked away. When present-day loss occurs, we may not be aware of remembering our growing up years, but we are certainly feeling the accumulated pain.

Tom, who was raised in an extremely critical home and felt his loss through chronic rejection, quickly separated from his parents and all his siblings after high school. Then, at the age of twenty-eight when his fiancée broke up with him, his exaggerated and catastrophic thinking led into incredible despair. He had talked himself into seeing himself as totally unworthy. He envisioned that his fiancée would marry someone much more financially stable than he was and certainly a lot more fun and exciting. She would have children with someone else. He would be alone all of his life. He was convinced he would never find happiness and he would never be able to offer anything to anyone else. On and on and on Tom's incredibly painful thinking continued. Soon, he was sleeping twelve to fourteen hours a day, missing days at work, and no longer exercising or eating properly.

Losing a relationship, particularly in young adulthood, happens to many of us. However, because of chronic losses in his childhood, Tom had not learned the skills needed to grieve through the loss of his fiancée. He was not able to understand the experience in any way except as further evidence of his inadequacy and worthlessness. This loss was simply one more that added fuel to his already existing fire of shame. Like victimization, depression is a consequence of the inability to defend and protect ourselves against the pain of loss.

Suicide: The Most Severe Response to Pain

"I am hopeless. I am unworthy and I don't deserve to live. Life won't get any better and I can't stand this pain." Suicidal thoughts, attempts, and completions speak of many issues. They are often a reflection of anger, rage turned inward, and depression. For some people, the act of suicide seems to grant power that compensates for the powerlessness in their life. For others, death is perceived to be a better option than living with certain memories and shame. The pain is too overwhelming and, out of despair and hopelessness, people become their own victims. Thoughts of taking our own lives are much more prevalent than people realize.While pain creates such thoughts, we also experience shame for having the thoughts. My message to you is, Please don't feel ashamed. But, please do speak up and let someone know how frightened, angry, or hopeless you are feeling.

In recovery, you can speak about those issues that have created the pain. You can say no to your shame. You can learn to find ways to express your anger without hurting yourself. You can develop new beliefs and behaviors that support you in the way you deserve to be supported.You can learn how to access the power within you that does exist.You deserve to be able to live without pain. But when you are considering suicide as a way out of your pain, you must reach out and get assistance from a helping professional.

BEHAVIORAL RESPONSES TO PAIN

"Medicating"Pain

Whether our emotional response to pain is one of victimization, rage, or depression, we may also try different behaviors to control our pain, hoping to lessen the hurt. Unfortunately, our efforts to control the pain don't remove the cause or source of our feeling. One way people try to control and regulate their pain is by "medicating" it through addiction to substances or compulsive behaviors.

Substance Addictions

Types of addictions may include dependency on food, caffeine, nicotine, sugar, alcohol, and other drugs. Many of the substances people become addicted to are socially sanctioned and supported, making it very difficult for the abuser to see how they are using them in unhealthy ways. In addition to temporarily controlling our pain, the substances we use and abuse very often provide something for us we do not know how to seek naturally. As an example, alcohol may give a sense of power to someone who has only known powerlessness. It may give access to a sense of courage and confidence to someone who feels lacking. This is certainly drug-induced, temporary and false, but for many people, false is better than none.

For someone who is isolated and feels alienated from others, alcohol makes it easier to reach out to people. "Give me a little bit to drink and I become alive. I pull myself away from the wall and I find myself talking, laughing, listening. I see people responding to me and I like it." This kind of thinking doesn't mean that a person is addicted, but it does mean he or she is thirsty for connection with others. In this case alcohol becomes the reinforcement in order to feel whole and complete.

For people who have never taken time for play or laughter because life has been so serious and "I have to get things done," alcohol gives them the opportunity to relax. Alice identified, "My entire life has been spent taking care of other people. I am always busy. I make these lists daily, thinking the world will stop if I don't get the job done. I don't think about missing out on fun—it has never been a part of my life. "I was a teetotaler. I never drank until I was twenty-six. I don't even know why I started. But those first few times I remember thinking that I was being silly, hearing myself laugh with other people. It actually scared me. Yet at the same time there was this attraction. It was as if there was this whole other part of me I didn't know and maybe was okay to know.

"The attraction to relaxing with alcohol kept getting stronger. I can actually remember thinking, 'I don't have to make this decision tonight,' or 'I don't have to do this by myself.' Pretty soon it was, 'I don't have to do this at all.' I was having fun. I was relaxing." Alice's new ways of letting go and becoming less rigid were not harmful, but because she did not know how to relax without alcohol she ultimately became dependent on it. Alice, like so many others, was seeking wholeness. But the only glimpse she had of it was "under the influence."

Variations of this scenario fit for other addictions. Our relationship to certain foods or the intake, lack of intake, and/or purging of food may be about an internal struggle with power and control. We may be attempting to access power that we don't have the skills or confidence to access more naturally. Starving ourselves, purging, and compulsive overeating may be anger turned toward ourselves. Possibly we are punishing ourselves for being bad. The anorexic may be literally starving herself to become invisible in response to shame; the anorexic and bulimic may be seeking perfection— which is based in shame. When we come from a pain-based family, it is common to go outside of ourselves for a quick answer to relieve our suffering. It doesn't seem possible that we have any way to help ourselves. Yet, ultimately, we can keep our pain under control only so long before it starts to leak out. Frightened, we feel out of control and we seek a medicator. Sometimes that medicator is a person or possibly an activity; many times it is a substance. Often it is a combination of compulsions and addictions.

Compulsions

To experience shame and powerlessness is to be in unbearable pain. While physical pain is horrible, there are moments of relief. There is hope of being cured. However, when we believe we are defective, there is no cure. Shame is a defeated state. We have no relationship with ourselves or anyone else; we are totally alone. Relief from this intolerable pain must come, one way or another. We need someone or something to take away our profound loneliness and fear, and so we seek a mood-altering experience. We need an escape. Everyone has certain behaviors used as a way to "escape," but it is when we come to depend on them to relieve our unworthiness that these become compulsive in nature. And when we grow up in an environment of shaming, where the cause of pain is external, we develop the belief that the solutions to problems exist only externally through substances or behaviors that are medicators.

There are many different types of addictions and compulsions ranging from compulsively repeated activities to preoccupying thoughts to relationship dependencies. We may use some form of keeping busy to distance or to distract ourselves, to get our minds off our pain, our fear, or our anger. We keep busy to stay in control of our feelings and therefore to avoid feeling bad. Many behavioral compulsions would be otherwise harmless activities if they weren't exaggerated, destroying the balance in our lives. For example, exercise is a healthy activity until done so excessively that we actually injure our bodies. Relationship addiction is the dependence on being in a relationship to validate our worth. That means we use other people to lessen our shame and to avoid truly facing our selves. Sex addiction is the use of sexual stimulation to act as a detractor or medicator of pain; or it may be a false way of accessing power to overcome our sense of powerlessness. Compulsive sex experiences can temporarily offer us warmth and an appearance of love. Or we can act out sex as an expression of anger. These sex experiences may temporarily affirm that we are lovable and worthy, all the while compounding our belief in our defectiveness. Sex addicts vary in their focus, from obsessive masturbating, the use of pornographic materials, exhibitionism, obscene phone calls, voyeurism, to multiple affairs, use of prostitutes, and so on. For sex addicts, certain behaviors take on sexual meaning. They view objects and people through their sexual preoccupation.

Even though compulsive behaviors distract and alter feelings, feelings themselves can become compulsive in nature. We become dependent on certain feelings to mask and avoid experiencing what we are really feeling. We may become a rage-aholic, using rage as a release for all feelings. Fear can overwhelm us, where phobias, hyper-vigilance, and/or anxieties can control our lives. While some compulsions are certainly more harmful to ourselves and our family, others may be considered only nuisances. Substances and behaviors can detract from our pain and, therefore, represent attempts to control whether or not we feel such pain. Yet any time we use a substance or become involved in a process or behavior that interferes with our honesty, our ability to be present with ourselves, it deserves our attention.

RATIONAL OR COGNITIVE RESPONSES TO PAIN

While some people focus on controlling the pain itself, others attempt to control the source of the pain. Control is the key word here. These people hope to control the cause of the pain, as opposed to removing, releasing, or healing it. As with the emotional and behavioral responses discussed earlier, these cognitive or rational responses try to prevent potential abandonment and prevent the possibility of exposing a shameful self.

Perfectionism

A common rational or cognitive response to pain is perfectionism. Perfectionism is driven by the belief that if a person's behavior is perfect there will be no reason to be criticized and therefore no more cause for pain. However, perfectionism is a shame-based phenomenon because children learn that "no matter what they do, it's never good enough." As a result, in their struggle to feel good about themselves and relieve the source of pain, they constantly push to excel, to be the best.

Highly perfectionistic people are usually people who have been raised in a rigid family environment. The rigidity may be in the form of unrealistic expectations that parents have for their children and/or for themselves. In these situations, the children internalize the parents' expectations. Also, rigidity may be expressed as children feel the need to do things "right" in order to gain approval from their parent and to lessen fears of rejection. For most children, being "right" is perceived to mean there is no room for mistakes.

Let's look at the example of Teri, nineteen years old, in a therapy group and talking about being a perfectionist. "When I was in junior high school, in order to be able to visit with friends on Saturday afternoon I had to complete certain household tasks. So, every Saturday morning I would approach my father to get a list of what I needed to accomplish to be able to go out later in the day. I'd pick up his typewritten list and go on about my duties. When the list was completed, I'd return it to my father, but then he just gave me a second list. When I was done with that list, I was inevitably given a third list. Many times there was a fourth and fifth list."

As you can guess, Teri didn't spend a lot of Saturday afternoons with her friends. When Teri told this story, tears streamed down her cheeks. Then she paused and reflectively commented, "But we all come from some pretty crazy families. It could have been worse. Besides, I learned a few things. If you want something done, ask me. I know how to be quick." Then haltingly she added, "What I really learned, though, was that no matter what

I do, it's never good enough." That was the lesson for Teri. No matter what she did, it wasn't good enough. Nothing was good enough because it wasn't humanly possible to please her father. This Saturday ritual was not about Teri. It was about her father and his need to control, his need for power. Whether or not Terri was permitted to spend time with her friends was not about how well or how quick she was in her work. For her own well-being, Teri would need to acknowledge that. In doing so, she would be able to establish an emotional boundary, separating her worth from her father's severe criticism. In doing this she would be saying no to the shame she had internalized that told her she wasn't good enough. She can then start to counter the shame-based message by acknowledging her worth.

Unfortunately, most perfectionists have no internal sense of limits. With shame and fear nipping at their heels the entire time, they always perceive their performance as related to a standard or judgment outside themselves. As children, they were taught to strive onward. There was never a time or place to rest or to have inner joy and satisfaction. Perfection as a performance criteria means you never measure up. Then, not measuring up is translated into a comparison with others of good versus bad, better versus worse. Inevitably you end up feeling the lesser for the comparison. Comparison with others is one of the primary ways that people continue to create more shame for themselves. You continue to do to yourself on the inside what was done to you from the outside. Since your efforts were never experienced as sufficient, adequate, or good enough, you did not develop an internal sense of how much is good enough.

As adults, we need to identify those areas where we once strived so hard for recognition, attention, and approval. Then we need to come to the understanding that not only did we do our best, but we truly were good enough. The lack of acceptance we have felt is not about us or our worth, but a residue left from those who judged us and who sought power by threatening to reject us. While we were not able to understand that as children, we can come to terms with that today.

Procrastination and Ambivalence

Procrastination, such as starting but not completing a project, or considering a project but never initiating it, is often an attempt to defend against further shame. Perfectionism and procrastination are closely linked. It is easy to picture Teri, in the example given, never finishing her first list, realizing that she could not please her father. Teri, though, believed in herself a bit more strongly than most people who procrastinate. Often, the procrastinator has little confidence and more fear. The perfectionist is more apt to follow through because there is the possibility of the reinforcement of some sense of accomplishment. The procrastinator will not even see that possibility. Some children received so little attention that they were not encouraged to initiate projects, let alone complete them. Too many times when these children did something, drew a picture or wrote a story and gleefully showed their parents, the parents barely looked at it and then set it aside, or maybe even lost it. When there is no positive reinforcement to complete school projects or homework, children perform with ambivalence. They believe that "No one else cares" and develop the attitude, "Why should I care?" The result is procrastination and ambivalence.

It was just as painful for children when their parents did pay attention, but were constantly critical, maybe making a joke of the children's work, possibly humiliating them in front of others. Sue, who was an average student in school, became very excited about a history project during her sophomore year of high school. "I worked hard on it all quarter, which was unusual for me, but I found this real interesting and the teacher liked me. For the first time in a long time I really wanted to do something well. One night I was at the dining room table putting all of the pages of my report in a notebook to be turned in the next day in class. I wasn't expecting my parents to come home for a few hours yet, so I was shocked when my mother and stepfather came in, both laughing loudly, both drunk. Mom asked what I was doing and then picked up my paper which was titled 'Did

America Need To Be In World War II?' Suddenly, she was in a rage and calling me a communist, saying I wasn't patriotic. "It was unreal. Within minutes, they were both screaming at me, calling me all kinds of names. They took my report and, in their words, threw the 'trash' into the fireplace. Well, there was no way I could tell the teacher what had happened. I just took a failing grade. It was pretty horrifying, but I should have known not to put that much effort into anything. Most things never worked out for me too much." Sue's sense of defeat was a culmination of similar experiences. Whenever she put forth effort to achieve, she somehow always felt diminished. It was several years before she could put into perspective the report incident and all the smaller incidents that led her to believe even if she wanted to work at something, it probably wasn't worth the effort. As a result, Sue quit trying to achieve at a very young age.

When children are humiliated for their efforts, made to feel inadequate or stupid, they find ways to protect themselves so they cease involvement in any action that would prove they really are a failure. In addition, children become discouraged when they are constantly compared to someone who "did it better" or might have done it better. Tom says he was always compared to his two older brothers. "My two older brothers were articulate. They were quick and did well in school. It took me longer to grasp things. I wasn't as interested in math and sciences as they were. I was more interested in my friends. So, with school being more of a struggle and having no real help from my parents, only the push that 'you should be like your brothers,' I just gave up. I wasn't like them and didn't want to be."

Also mixed into procrastination can be anger, expressed as an attitude of "I'll show you—I won't finish this," or "I'll only do it part way. I won't give my best." Inherent in this attitude is a challenge that insists, "Like me for who I am, not for what I do." In a family where rigidity is the rule, where it is not okay to make mistakes, not okay to take risks or be different, not okay to draw attention to yourself, you learn not to initiate, or not to finish what you started. For those of us raised this way, it is amazing that we get anything done. Our pain, our choice of responses, and the consequences of our choices are summarized on the chart, "From a Past of Chronic Loss to the Turning Point: The Experience of Pain from an Adult's Point of View."

Understanding Your Defenses Against Pain

Rage, depression, victimization, addictions, compulsions, perfectionism, and procrastination—these are some of the responses to having lived with fear and pain. Such responses often become protectors. They offer ways to control the pain itself and/or control the source of the pain. Other protectors begin as common, everyday acts, but taken to extremes create negative outcomes in the long run. Some of these are intellectualization, physical isolation, humor, magical thinking, lying, silence, and withdrawal.

Letting Go of the Past, Healing the Pain

Every one of us would like to rid ourselves of pain. The answer lies in being willing to admit and show your pain. That means facing the feelings. It means being willing to own the sadness, the hurt and the fears, embarrassments and anger about how you have had to live your life. It means being willing to be specific about all the ways you fought for emotional survivorship, how you attempted to compensate for powerlessness, and how you tried to gain control to overcome the incredible sense of shame and fear that has been so significant in your life.

We Can't Go Forward Without Finishing the Past

To go forward, we must finish and let go of the past. Jill Johnston, author of Mother Bound, writes that as we let go of the past, "we alter the way we see ourselves in the present and the way we cast ourselves into the future. . . . The notion of who has rights, whose voice can be heard, whose individuality is worthy, comes under revision . . . and the shame of difference will evaporate."

To let go of our pain, we must also acknowledge what we have been doing in the present to control our pain. Facing our own painful reality, both past and present, empowers us by giving us choice. One option is that we can remain role players, acting out old family roles, directed by negative judgments and false beliefs about ourselves. Choosing this option, of course, we are not really attempting to finish the past. Also, we are consigning ourselves to a future weighted down by the need to manage our shame and pain. The other option we have is to become free agents, choosing to set our own course and act according to our own freely chosen beliefs, rather than the dictates of external standards. On this course we are able to finish the past because we are no longer being controlled by it.

Finishing the past does not mean that it disappears from our memories. Instead, it simply takes its rightful place as one significant dimension of our personal history. Letting go of our pain doesn't mean that we will, or should, forget our suffering. That would be another kind of denial. In time we can learn to honor our past pain much as we would honor a soldier returning from war. We can also honor our experience as a significant part of our life's struggle to grow and survive.

Freeing ourselves from pain is what recovery is all about. Releasing ourselves from the past and freeing ourselves from the painful limitations of our past-driven present life is the process we go through as we turn to the new reality we want. Remember that recovery takes time. But it can be done. It can happen to you, to me, to all of us.

We are much, much more than mere embodiments of pain. Realizing that truth allows us to separate our selves from our emotional responses.

Further, our own response is something we can affect, something we can make a choice about. As Steven Covey writes, "Responsibility is response-ability."

Together, these awarenesses lead us to the turning point that can put us on the path of freedom:

- Our pain is our responsibility.
- What we do about our pain is a choice we make.

CHAPTER 3

BUILDING YOUR OWN INNER ADULT

Although the specifics are different in everyone's lives, we do know a great deal about the dynamics that are common within troubled families. We know that something, some event or some force, has disrupted the natural order of lives. An event might be the absence/loss of a parent through death or divorce, a parent's debilitating depression, or drastically reduced living conditions for the family. A force might be as blatantly harmful as drug addiction, or subtle and deceptively benign—a strict religious code of behavior, for example.

In the midst of chaos, rigidity, or a combination of the extremes, and in the absence of strong, positive parental messages to the contrary, children conclude that they are not of value and that they may at any time be abandoned. These two things in combination are the source of almost unbearable shame. We are often desperate in our attempts to hide our core self because we feel damaged or loathsome. Unbeknown to us, other children had early daily encounters with loving, nurturing mothers and fathers, so they felt both physically and emotionally safe. They were able to internalize memories of being cared for, which then formed their core beliefs about and behaviors toward themselves. These core beliefs and behaviors are the ones we will have to learn on our own because, as Judith Viorst writes, "We cannot stand alone until we come to possess this inner holding environment."

The core beliefs and behaviors that create this "inner holding environment" are the core recovery skills, built around a core of positive regard for ourselves and the willingness to nurture our inner being.

CORE RECOVERY SKILLS

New awareness of what is possible can bring you to the turning point in your life. You can change course. It is very important to remember, though, that you are not changing who you are. You are changing certain beliefs and behaviors—you are changing how you see yourself and how you take care of your pain! Using the Four Steps to Recovery discussed in chapter 3, you will have a basic understanding of how your past has been affecting your life and how you can challenge and change old beliefs and behaviors for your present and future. Now you are ready to learn the skills you need to take care of yourself on your course to recovery.

Core Recovery Skills

1. Validate yourself
2. Let go of some control
3. Feel your feelings
4. Identify your needs
5. Set limits and boundaries

These are the skills that everyone needs but which you did not learn because, whether all or in part, these were missing when you were growing up. Because you did not receive validation, you did not feel of value. With a child's logic, you concluded that you were not worthy. During the very early stages of your development, and without other messages to the contrary, there was no way for you to conclude anything else. The family is the be all and end all to children's experiences until they get old enough and mature enough to conceive of other possibilities.

When chaos prevailed—because of a raging alcoholic or because parents were literally absent in the home for whatever reason—your physical survival was in jeopardy. When rigidity was the order, your emotional survival, and possibly your physical survival, were at risk since severe punishment often followed misbehavior. Whatever the case in your family, whether it be chaos, rigidity, or some other extreme, the first priority was, literally, to save yourself. So you tried in every way possible to be in control of what happened to you and others who were at risk.

Of course, when you were discounted, shamed, or punished, you simply hid your feelings, and then kept hiding them deeper and deeper until you didn't seem to feel them any more. Along with no longer recognizing your own feelings, you also learned to ignore your needs. After all, your parents' needs and wants came first. If your parents or others in your family were sucked into a system of addiction and codependency, children were simply caught up in following the rules of protection and denial, as well as caretaking the parents and themselves. If the central dynamic of the system was some kind of obsession with a religious code, children's needs were probably not acknowledged as legitimate and any deviance from that code was a sin.

Whatever was true in your family, others set your limits and tried to invade the boundaries of your core self and perhaps the boundaries of your physical self. Inevitably, these intrusions were confusing and painful. Today you are, in essence, becoming your own parent. In truth, we all parent ourselves when we become adults. We have internalized beliefs and behaviors that either echo our parents or stand in opposition to them, as we try to compensate for the negative effects we felt. Rather than look back in anger at what we did and didn't learn, or look with envy at what others did learn, we can simply begin with the premise that all of us act as either loving or unloving parents to ourselves now. Parenting ourselves is a concept that feels artificial to some and off-putting to others—maybe because we have negative memories of being parented and so that's the last thing we want to go through again. However, let's not get stuck in the connotations of the words parent and child. Let's just take a careful look at how we treat ourselves. We either put ourselves down or build ourselves up; we treat ourselves badly or we take care of ourselves.

But now, we can consciously decide what we want to do for ourselves or, if you will, what kind of parent we want to be. We can decide what we want to believe and feel and do about ourselves—and go from there.

"Passion and Gradualness"

Taking steps one at a time is a natural learning process that builds on itself. If we jump into situations before we learn how to handle them we won't be able to reach our goals. For example, we may hope to have intimacy in our relationships but we may not have learned yet how to express our feelings. Or, we want to be the perfect parent but we never learned how to set limits for ourselves, let alone our children. However, rather than be hard on ourselves for wanting too much, too soon, we can remind ourselves that, according to Albert Schweitzer, all great enterprises—and rebuilding our lives is certainly a great enterprise—require two things, "passion and gradualness." Being raised in a troubled family often meant being raised in a family where your sense of safety was unsure. You couldn't trust that you were going to be physically protected. Because of that, you didn't feel psychologically safe. You didn't feel the protection that children need to experience in order to be willing to risk assertive behavior. You didn't feel the protection children need to experience to be willing to risk sharing what they feel and need. Safety to share and to risk are elements that nurture a person's growth. It is my hope that as you change course now, you will find recovery to be a safe process. That does not mean your life will be pain free or necessarily easy, but that you will feel safe to risk and grow.

There are different ways that people approach recovery, just as there are different ways to learn other skills. Take swimming, as an example. If I wanted to teach children to swim there are many ways to do that. It is possible to take children out on a raft in water ten feet over their heads, throw them over the side, and expect them to swim back to shore. While many children would make it back to shore, it is very possible a few would not and would be in danger of drowning. This is a harsh and unnecessary way to learn.

The recovery process does not need to be so harsh. Don't be in a rush to jump into recovery situations that are ten feet over your head. When you've learned and acquired core recovery skills you will have built the foundation for your "inner holding environment." Practicing these skills will allow you to face the core causes of your pain without feeling like you will drown in your emotions. It is as if you are learning to swim with a sense of safety, starting in shallow waters and developing your self-confidence as you go deeper.

It is my hope that early on in recovery you quickly begin to practice self validation and self-approval. This paves the way for you to feel safer as you explore more fully the issues of control, confronting your need to stay in control and learning to let go little by little. Letting go of control quickly results in immediately being thrust into the issue of dealing with powerful feelings. At the point you begin to identify and express feelings you will also start to identify your needs. Then, to get needs met, you must begin to set limits and boundaries. As you do these things, you are developing a sense of self—a sense of who you really are. Self-worth is increasing. Shame is lessening. A foundation of positive self-regard is being constructed.

This foundation will offer you the safety to go to greater depths within yourself, which in turn will take you further on the course of your recovery. As you proceed to build the strength of your inner core you will undoubtedly still be frightened of letting go of some control. With this and other very difficult issues, I want you to have some comfort with your feelings. If you start to cry, I want you to know that you are not going crazy. And if you are angry, you don't have to self-destruct. I want you also to be able to identify what you need.

Very often people feel the need to jump into all of their issues at once,

and that is like experiencing "emotional" or "cognitive" surgery without medical help or preparation. When this occurs, the consequences are so frightening that people often just stop their efforts to work through their pain. They may become so afraid of what they are feeling that they won't risk continuing. By taking steps one at a time, the "gradualness" provides the safety to continue in the process. At the same time, these recovery skills can't really be worked on in a totally compartmentalized fashion. You cannot do all the work that is necessary in one area—validating yourself, for example—before moving on to another skill, such as identifying your needs. Human emotions are not that simple, and human behavior is not constant or absolute. Our issues will easily overlap and working through them will require different skills in different combinations. Yet, when we set out to learn the skills, the concept of doing the steps of recovery in order is still valid.

Validating Yourself

We need to gain a sense of value in order to feel we are worthy of the recovery process. As soon as possible, we must begin the process of actively valuing and approving ourselves. A part of recovery is to become independent of the need for other people's approval. Many people raised in troubled families are often highly dependent upon others' approval and on what others think of them. It is important to become self-validating so that we are not so dependent on others, but also because it allows us to see movement in our process of recovery. It allows us to see that, in fact, we are doing things differently now than we have done them in the past. It allows us to see our progress, and that gives us something to celebrate. It also gives us a sense of hope, direction, and helps to keep us in the process.

Yet, most of us are harshly critical of ourselves. Unless we do something as significant as moving a mountain, it is never good enough. And then if we do move the mountain, unless there are people there applauding, it is still never good enough. Few people in their lifetimes ever move mountains, but if they do, they do it with the help of a lot of other people and by taking a lot of little steps. Yet, it isn't the mountain getting moved that makes the difference—it is the little steps along the way.

Earlier I mentioned the tendency for people to take recovery in leaps and bounds. This is understandable because so much of our life has been experienced in extremes and with unrealistic expectations. We have often lived our life from a "one and ten" perspective (forgetting the numbers two through nine)—an all or nothing way of being, feeling, living. We need to accept and validate ourselves for being who we are. Because we can never be perfect, we are not doomed to failure. We must accept both our power and powerlessness in life.

We deserve to experience our personal growth, to celebrate and feel good about ourselves. Yet, it is so difficult to be self-approving when, as a child, you learned that no matter what you did, it was never good enough. We don't need anyone today to reinforce this belief/delusion; we have internalized it.We have been constantly repeating that message to ourselves. As children we needed our parents to tell us specifically what was likable or lovable about us. We needed our parents to applaud us for just being. Parents are often critical of their children, very abrupt in their responses, and often simply don't notice the little things (or even the big things) that help children feel good about who they are. One child comes home from school, looking forward to telling her mother about the day, to find Mom passed out on the couch. Another child comes home to tell his mother something that made him feel good that day and finds Mom locked inside the bedroom crying. In either case, the children aren't going to be acknowledged, supported, or validated. Their needs are ignored, and they are recognized only when they try to take care of their mother.

Another child brings home his report card that shows he has done extremely well. He is anxious to show it to Dad, seeking Dad's approval, but Dad doesn't come home that night. In fact, three days go by before Dad returns. Do you think anyone remembers then that this thirteen-year-old boy has brought home his report card? Does anyone care? No, everybody is focused on Dad—where he had been, what he was doing, and what will happen now.

When children are developing their sense of worth and their identity, they gain a sense of their personal value by others' verbal responses, or failure to respond, and others' behavior toward them. Children need to know what is good about their behavior and themselves. "I need to know that I am special. I am of value. I am important." They consistently need to hear words that affirm this. When that does not occur, children fail to internalize a sense of worth, value, or accomplishment. As an adult, you need to begin validating yourself as a part of your own reparenting process. When people truly begin to validate themselves simply for being who they are, they are not going to have to continue to seek outside approval.

When you first begin to look back at your early loss conditions, such as the absence of validation, it is easy to get overwhelmed by personal pain. Consequently, people often comment they wish they were still in denial. People talk about entering the tunnel of recovery and, rather than seeing light at the end, feel the tunnel closing in around them, getting darker. If this happens to you, it may help to remember this:

You deserve to have a sense of moving forward. You deserve self validation and self-approval. This will give you a sense of hope and give you the patience that you deserve to help you work through your losses. I want you to be able to validate yourself so you can say: "Today someone asked my opinion and I had one. Yes, me! I—who have never felt safe forming my own opinion—I had one."

"Today I got angry and I knew it. In the past it took me six years to figure out I had a feeling and another two years to know it was anger." "I didn't work through my whole lunch hour, just half of it." "Today I received a compliment. I said thank you and didn't say 'Yes, but. . . .'"

Affirming, approving, validating—these are the little steps for which you deserve applause. It is very important to stop and take time to identify the little steps in recovery, the little bits of success. This strengthens your sense of self and reinforces your new beliefs. Also, try not to be preoccupied with what hasn't changed for you yet. Focus on what is happening now. Start now—lay this book down, stand up, and applaud yourself! You are in the process of recovery.

As a way of making self-validation a habit, take time out each day to focus on your positive attributes. Recognize at least three new behaviors or attitudes that are reflective of your real, valuable self and the new direction you are taking.

Here is an example of the four recovery steps applied to self-validation.

Step One: Describe how validation was or was not experienced in your growing up years. How did that feel? Be willing to feel the pain associated with those experiences.

Step Two: Identify how the experience you had regarding validation in your growing up years has affected your willingness and ability to self validate today.

Step Three: Identify specific beliefs you have internalized about the act of self-validation. Are these beliefs hurtful or helpful to you today? Identify the ones you want to let go of and those you would like to maintain.

Step Four: Begin to practice the skill of validating yourself, for example, by repeating, "I am a whole human being with a wide range of thoughts and feelings. I accept and love myself—my body, my thoughts, my feelings— just the way that I am, and I know that I am worthy." Make a list of affirmations that are true for yourself. Keep them with you at all times and periodically throughout the day pull them out and say them. Get to the point that you don't need your list but can draw upon the skill of spontaneously acknowledging that which you can feel good about.

LETTING GO OF SOME CONTROL

Most of us adults know a lot about the word control, but those of us raised in either chaotic or rigid environments know very little about the word some, S-O-M-E, as in "some control." To us, control has been something we either have or we don't. The concept of "some control" has seemed as impossible as being "a little bit pregnant." Perceiving control to be an all-or-nothing experience, naturally we don't want to give it up. That would be the same, we believe, as being "out of control." Also, we don't want to give up control because it once protected us. Giving up control is frightening because it has been vital to our sense of safety. Control of the external forces in your environment is a survival mechanism. It may be self-protection in a physical sense. Or, from the standpoint of your beliefs and feelings, control is what allowed you, when you were a young child, to make sense out of your life. Controlling behavior is an attempt to bring order and consistency into inconsistent and unpredictable family situations. Controlling behavior is a defense against shame. Feeling a sense of control gives children a sense of power at a time in their lives when they are overwhelmed with powerlessness, helplessness, and fears. Giving up control as an adult is difficult when, up to this point in life, it has been of great value.

One way children learn control is by manipulating their environment. They try to control the aspects of their lives that are tangible or concrete. You can see this when children act as their own parent, and/or as the parent to their brothers and sisters. Sometimes they act as a parent to their mother and father.

Susan said she actually used to discipline herself for having misbehaved. "I would do things and not be reprimanded. I talked back to my parents. I would swear. Maybe I would be late for school. So I would discipline myself. I put myself on restriction. I would role-play verbal reprimands. I used television shows as my guide. I actually raised myself fairly well." At eleven years of age, Tim was the one who set the bedtime for his younger brother and sister. He made sure they had a bath before they went to bed. He literally tucked them in himself. He then made sure their lunches were made before school the next morning.

Fourteen-year-old Kimberly used to call her father to tell him what he needed to do before he came home from work. This same youngster was the one who covered her mother up after she passed out on the couch, so that she wouldn't get too cold during the middle of the night.

Ten-year-old Paul put the car in the garage every night when his dad would leave it running in the middle of the front yard. He didn't want the neighbors to think there was anything wrong at his house. These are examples of children trying their best to create order and safety in their lives. While many children try to control that which is external—people, places, and things—they may also attempt to control internal, intangible aspects of their personal lives. Some children become very controlling by withholding their feelings. Discounting their feelings usually goes along with this.

"I'm not angry. What's there to be angry about? I've seen it before."

"I wasn't embarrassed. I'm used to those things by now."

"No, I didn't feel sad. Last time I cried, they called me names."

Some children become very controlling by diminishing their own needs, neither expecting nor asking for anything.

"I don't need to go to my friend's house. Who would be home to take care of my sister?"

"I don't want a birthday party. Dad wouldn't show up anyway."

"I don't want my mom to come to the PTA meeting. Last time she showed up, it was a major fiasco."

Diminishing needs and withholding feelings are invisible, internal controlling mechanisms. This is self-control, protection to ward off further pain by repressing desires and feelings. Some children become very controlling through withdrawal and isolation. They go off in the corner and read. They daydream in their bedroom or, when teenagers, spend as little time at home as possible. They establish a social boundary that says, "Stay away. I don't need you. I don't want you. Let me go do something alone in safety that keeps me from the depth of my painful feelings."

Because of their early experiences, people do differ in the depth of their control and in the ways they control. However, in my work, I have consistently observed some commonalities.

1.   The greater the physical and emotional chaos in a family, the greater a child will find the need for control in every area of his or her life.

2.   The faster the dysfunction in a family progresses and deepens, the less a child becomes an external controller and instead becomes more of an internal controller.

3.   When another family member is already an external controller, there is less need for another child to be an external controller, and so more often that child will learn to control internally only.

4.   External controllers also control internally, but some people are only internal controllers.

When we were children, our attempts to control, whether internally or externally, were about survivorship. It made sense in the context of our environment. Unfortunately, the continued need for control causes problems in our adult lives. We have spent years being hyper-vigilant, manipulating others and ourselves as a way of protection. Now we literally don't know how to live life differently. We don't have any idea why we would want to live life differently. Because we have survived, our ways have apparently been right.

Unfortunately, because we have become so encapsulated and narrow in our view of the world, we don't see what others can so readily see—that we have become rigid, authoritarian, demanding, inflexible, and perfectionistic. We don't know how to listen. We cut people off in conversations and relationships. We don't ask for help. We can't see options. We have little spontaneity or creativity. We experience psychosomatic health problems. We intimidate people by withholding our feelings.

Blindly focused on our pursuit of safety, very often unaware of our emotional self, and yet so frightened and full of shame, we rely on what we know best—control. But the consequences are almost the opposite of what we had hoped for. Our needs do not get met. Our relationships are out of balance. Ultimately, our hyper-vigilance becomes burdensome and exhausting.

Sadly, we don't know how to go about life any differently. In our confusion about what has gone wrong when we've tried so hard to make things right, we succumb to depression and/or resort to unhealthy ways to cope with sadness and pain that often results in addictive behaviors. While some people don't identify with having tried to be in control in their lives during their growing up years, they will often speak of how strongly controlling one or both of their parents were, which indicates that the children were victims of control. When these young people grow up they usually react in one of two ways. They may assume a victim position in adulthood, continuing to be in relationship to others who are highly controlling, or they will most likely seek control in every area of life to make up for the lack of personal power they experienced. They are usually at least somewhat conscious of their efforts to have power and mastery over everything in life. They are frequently blatantly angry, though they fail to acknowledge the anger. Typically, their anger is tightly controlled. Very often that anger is a direct response to a parent's controlling relationship.

Adults react to chronic parental control in many ways. For example, people with a food disorder are controlling what does and does not go into their mouth, trying to compensate for the powerlessness they had over the abusive control they experienced. Another example can be seen when one person in a relationship dominates the other, as a result of the anger felt toward the highly controlling parent of the opposite sex. In other words, a woman would dominate her husband in order to act out her anger at her controlling father. Whether or not we have sought control to make up for the lack of control in our lives, fear and shame are the factors that fuel our need to seek control.

Ways We Try to Control

People demonstrate control in a variety of ways, but the following four postures illustrate particularly common ways people disguise their conscious or unconscious attempts to control:

Sweet Controller—This person is polite, pleasant, and sweet in order to get what she or he wants. We often respond positively to this person, attracted to her seeming innocence, or his charming smile, but in reflection we recognize all we know about them is how sweet they are. We realize we have become, often one more time, a part of a "one up/one down" relationship and we are in the one down role. Know, though, that sweetness by itself does not equate to being controlling. It is a lovely virtue. In the context of controlling behavior, however, sweetness is the guise under which one finds control.

Distant Controller—This is the person who is rigidly efficient, emotionally cold, and who develops a sense of mastery by paying attention to detail. A person like this is great to have in your life when you need a "detail person," but is difficult to be close to.

Passive Controller—This person is known to many as the Martyr, as is reflected by the words, "I don't care. Do whatever you want. You are more important than I am. Anyway, it doesn't matter to me." The control attempt lies in the unspoken intent, "But I'll get you in the end!"

Angry Controller—This person is an intimidator, who says to the world, "I want what I want, when I want it, and I will get it!" What all controllers have in common is that they operate from a basis of fear. Their fear has been so great that it has led to their need to protect themselves by staying in control. As a result, they have become disrespectful of other people's needs and boundaries. Ultimately, virtually all controllers will become angry. This is inevitable because they are going through life unable to get their needs met.

As controllers, all that we know about is "all or nothing" and "one or ten. "We fail to see that almost nothing in real life is on a "one or ten" basis, but that nearly everything lies in a continuum between the numbers two through nine. So, our experience in life is that we are in total control—or we have just lost it! When we feel our tight hold on control threatened, we scramble to regain control in any way we know. Yet, if we want to experience recovery, we must let go of some control.

Willingness to give up control is vital to being willing to engage in the recovery process, but this is not something you learn to do all at once. It is not an all-or-nothing process. As one gives up control it is okay to practice giving up control in those areas that feel psychologically safe. You may begin to practice letting go of control more easily in one setting than another. You may begin by "letting go" of which store you shop in, which movie you see, or who chooses which route you take on a trip. The more you practice "letting go," the easier it will become to begin gradually giving up control in the areas that cause the greatest pain, such as past loss conditions or present self-destructive behaviors.

Control Still Feels Like a Matter of Life and Death

Why are we so afraid of giving up control? We need to know what our belief is before we can challenge it and put it into perspective. For most of us, control still represents what it meant to us as children. If we grew up with chronic loss, then "giving up control" is often equated with "being out of control. "When I ask adults what not being in control would have meant to them as children, their answers include a wide range of painful memories such as:

- chaos, confusion
- being abandoned
- being left alone
- not being noticed
- being called names
- more anger, fear, sadness
- getting hit
- not being valued
- dying, death

Some people feared theirs or another's physical death. For others, it was emotional death and/or spiritual death, the death of their inner child's spirit. While the above responses are perceptions of adults looking back on childhood, the beliefs have never left. You may be thirty-five years old, but when you experience loss of control it is experienced from the reference of being a child. Someone will be hit, be abandoned, or die. Yet, as people so often remind me, those beliefs from childhood no longer make sense. "After all," you may be thinking, "an adult should be able to think things through, so such fears would be childish." My response is: "Who is that speaking? "Where does that internalized "should" message come from? Clearly, it is an echo from a long time ago. What is involved here is the emotional vulnerability a person carries from childhood.

We aren't conscious of these fears—these are internalized fears imprinted deep within our emotional beings that we have never been able to address. Now is the time to do so. We need to explore what control has meant and put it into its proper perspective. The chart, "Continuum of Control," offers a useful portrayal of control on a continuum. Because the whole notion of control is so important, it may help you to take time to focus on what control symbolizes for you. Sit back in a comfortable seat and relax . . . Breathe deeply . . . Uncross your legs and arms . . . Gently close your eyes and reflect back in time to your growing up years.

Here is an example of the four recovery steps applied to the issue of control.

Step One: Describe ways you learned controlling behavior (externally and/or internally) and the feelings you had at that time, whether or not you expressed them. Be willing to feel the pain associated to those times.

Step Two: Identify how that past experience has had an impact on you and how it affects your relationships to others today.

Step Three: Identify specific beliefs you have internalized about the need to be in control, whether or not it is internal or external control. Are these beliefs hurtful or helpful to you today? Identify the ones you want to let go of and those you would like to maintain.

Step Four: Identify the areas in your life where you would like to begin to let go of some control. List them in the order of which is most safe (easiest) to the more scary (the more difficult). Begin with the safest (easiest). Share this with a person you trust. Allow them to walk through the process with you.

Feeling Your Feelings

In the process of exploring the issue of control, we quickly become aware of our feelings. And we do have so much to feel about. People will have feelings around every recovery issue. Without exploring and becoming more comfortable with your emotional self you will quickly become stuck in the process. With each feeling there are three areas that need to be looked at:

- Fear of the feeling
- Identification of the feeling
- Expression of the feeling

While many adults are fearful of feelings and incapable of identifying any feelings, other people are very clear about what it is they feel. Usually, though, that is when there is only one dominant emotion. Some people may walk through life and the only feeling they know is their anger, or for another the only feeling they know is their sadness. Others will only know their helplessness.

There are some people who appear to "only love life." They are never angry, sad, or frightened; they are always accepting, loving, and understanding. What is really going on for them is that they have successfully buried these feelings and, on occasion, such feelings burst to the surface in bouts of rage or are manifested in depression. To make lemonade out of a lemon is great, but to refuse to acknowledge the lemon ever existed is denial—denial of ourselves and our experiences. It is when we can own and accept our feelings, whether they are irritations, fears, sadnesses, joys, etc., that we are able to love life. To be whole, we want to be able to access a range of feelings. A part of recovery is learning to identify a wide range of feelings and then learn the appropriate expression of those feelings. Although no parents can be perfect role models, the role modeling we saw in our dysfunctional home was often distorted. Our models for expressing feelings were gleaned from people who denied feelings, contradicted our perception of reality, and generally could not express positive or negative feelings in healthy ways.

We often saw people rage in anger or walk away in silence, succumbing to their fear and helplessness. Many times our parents converted one feeling to another; that is, they became sad when angry and vice versa. They added further confusion when they told us we had nothing to be frightened of when we did. They told us we had no right to be angry but that we should feel grateful. We wanted so much to love our parents without reservation. Then something would happen. They would act in such hurtful ways that we couldn't totally love them, leaving us confused and feeling guilty. As a result of living with a distorted and twisted expression of feelings, we watched, learned, and repeated the same pattern. Before you can express certain feelings, you need to face your fears about what might happen if you do. In other words, what are you afraid might happen if, for example, you express dislike for your mother, or if you start to cry because your father left you? Typically, some of those fears are: (1) others won't like me; (2) people are going to be able to see how bad I really am; (3) people will perceive me as weak; (4) they are going to perceive me as vulnerable, and to me that is the same thing as being bad; (5) others will tell me that I have no reason for feeling this way; or (6) I will not be in control and that is not okay.

These fears were most likely valid at one time in your life. When you expressed an honest emotion, your parents and other caretakers may have responded with some kind of rejection, which felt like abandonment. We need to ask ourselves, "Is that still true today?" Sometimes we never ask and yet we operate on fears that are ten, twenty, or even many more years old. If we express our feelings in the presence of certain people and their response is negative, the question we need to ask ourselves is, "Do we want to believe that other person's judgment?" Or do we want to validate ourselves, relying on our own internal judgment and strengthening our core of positive self-regard? For a while we will feel anxious about these choices, so we need to confront these fears early in recovery to allow ourselves to be honest about who we are.

You may also have difficulty expressing feelings because you have difficulty identifying them. If so, you need to go back and work on learning to identify feelings. People from family systems that did not sanction the expression of feelings may honestly have difficulty recognizing that their clenched fists and tightly folded arms are signs of anger. Early in the process of exploring feelings, it is not uncommon to ask people how they are feeling and hear the reply, "I don't know." Many therapists perceive that response as resistance. However, it is my experience that the person probably doesn't know. This is known as psychic numbness, emotional anesthesia, or frozen feelings.

If you are able to identify your feelings and still not express them, that is often due to the fear of what might happen. In this case, your fear needs to be explored further to find the freedom to use your emotional skills. To summarize, if you find yourself stuck in the area of feelings, you need to assess the problem to see if it has to do with the (1) fear of feeling, (2) identification of the feeling, or (3) expression of the feeling. Remember, do not confuse doing your grief work with the issue of exploring feelings in general. Identifying obstacles in dealing with your feelings will help you develop the skills to do the grief work. At the same time, it will give you the skills to express your feelings in the present.

Feelings are cues and signals that tell us that we have a need. If we pay attention to the feeling, we can learn what it is that we need. For example, if you feel some discomfort and reflect on what you are experiencing, you may identify the feeling to be loneliness. Knowing when you are lonely is important and you can deal with that in the present. But if you do not listen and respectfully respond to the feeling, you may try to compensate with some counterproductive behaviors instead, such as overworking or overeating. It is also helpful to know how you have become accustomed to compensating for your feelings, because those compensatory behaviors are also cues that tell us what we are feeling and what we need. For instance, to recognize overeating as a cover-up for sadness helps you to identify an opportunity to change your feeling response. Many, many people run from their feelings with certain behaviors. Some people use work, exercise, or shopping to distract themselves. Others use food and alcohol to medicate.

Feelings are also indicators that help us set boundaries that provide safety for us. Expressing our feelings allows us to connect and bond with others. This is what allows us to experience intimacy. Our emotional self is significant and vital to the opportunity to experience meaning in life. Yet, that does not mean recovery is about sharing every feeling we experience. A sign of recovery is the ability to know what you feel when you feel it, to be comfortable with your emotional self, and then to be able to determine whether or not and with whom you share feelings.

Here is an example of the four recovery steps applied to feeling your feelings.

Step One: Identify the feelings you had growing up, then note which feelings were okay to express and which were not. What would happen when you tried to express the more non-safe feelings? What did you fear would happen? What did you then do with the feelings that were not able to be expressed? Share these awarenesses with someone you trust. Be open to feeling the pain associated with remembering these experiences.

Step Two: Describe how those childhood experiences impact you today.

Step Three: Identify specific beliefs you have internalized about feelings in general, and then specific feelings. Are these beliefs hurtful or helpful to you today? Identify the ones you want to let go of and those you would like to maintain.

Step Four: Create a feeling list, which names a variety of feelings. Take time out each day, stop, pull out your list, and ask yourself what you are feeling. Is there someone you can share the feeling(s) with at that time or later? Is there something you can do, such as journal writing or a brief relaxation exercise that can serve as an act of self care should you be having a vulnerable feeling?

Identifying Your Needs

Learning to identify our feelings accesses our ability to recognize our needs. In families marked by chronic loss, children's needs are not met. Adults don't focus on the children's needs and the children don't or can't, because they are too young and without adequate adult support and nurturance. And, as we've said, often the children were kept busy taking care of others. For many of us, this focus on others became a safety net, a part of our identity, that has carried over into our adult lives. The payoff is, "If I don't focus on me, I won't feel the depth of my helplessness and powerlessness." But, as a result of not knowing our needs, they don't get met. No wonder we are depressed, angry, or confused. "Me? Oh, I don't have any needs. No, I don't need anything." Needs is spoken as if it is a foreign or even a vulgar word for many of us.

Taking a look at your needs can be as frightening as the idea of looking at your control issues. You will have to let go of some control before you can actively wrestle with the concept of having needs. You will need a strong sense of what your feelings are because your feelings are cues and signals that are critical to help identify needs. You are going to have to believe more in your own worth and that you deserve to have your needs met. It is easy for people to get caught up in the semantics of the word "needs." In grade school we were taught we only have five basic needs—air, food, clothing, shelter, and water—and everything else is a "want." This was presented as the basis for physical survival. The life you are now rebuilding is not only about physical existence—it is about going beyond.

Our psychological, emotional, social, and spiritual needs are that which give meaning to life. When needs are attended to, children learn skills that allow them to grow emotionally and psychologically, that allow them to move into adulthood with a sense of belonging, a sense of value, and a sense of competence. Regardless of your original parenting, it is no longer going to be your mother or father who will meet your needs. While your needs may not have been met as a child, you have an opportunity to meet your needs now. A major part of recovery is taking responsibility for meeting your needs. If your needs include establishing new relationships, it will mean finding people in your adult life today who respond to you in a positive, caring manner. This is about reparenting the child that is still within you.

Because many of us were given strong reinforcement for diminishing and not looking at our needs, we need to confront the concept of selfishness. "Is it okay for my needs to be important? Is it okay for my needs to be more important to me than other people's needs at this particular time?" Ellen, daughter of two alcoholic parents, married to her third alcoholic husband, was in a counseling session. When she was asked, "What do you need?" Ellen looked at the therapist, confused. She then looked away as if she had answered the question and was ready to move on. The therapist said, "Ellen, you have been taking care of other people all of your life. You took care of your parents, three husbands, and two children. It is time to take care of you. What do you need?" Ellen, clearly agitated, looked quickly away as if looking for the door. It was obvious she wanted to change the subject. Once again, the therapist said, "Ellen, Ellen, what do you need? Not anyone else, but you." This time Ellen's eyes opened wide and her body began to jerk; her knees jerked up and down; her head jerked slightly back, as if she were going to convulse. Being frightened, the therapist reached out, grabbing Ellen where she was twitching the most, at the knee and shoulder. As she was touching Ellen, she very calmly, yet firmly spoke to

Ellen saying, "Ellen, it is over. It is all over. You don't have to take care of anyone else. You only have to take care of you."

The twitching subsided. The therapist purposely pushed the obviously very loaded issue and again asked, "Ellen, what do you need?" Quietly, Ellen responded, "Need? What do I need? In my forty-four years, when has it ever been safe for me to ask myself what it is I need?" It had never been safe for Ellen to consider her needs. Her priority had always been feeling a sense of responsibility for others who were not taking responsibility for themselves. Now, it would be important for Ellen to recognize her own needs as an adult in order for them to be met. But, before she would be able to do that effectively, she would need to take a look at what the issue of "having needs" had meant her entire life, beginning with her growing up years.

While many adults like Ellen don't recognize they have needs, many others compartmentalize their needs, rejecting those needs that would involve others. This is the case when someone operates from the attitude, "I don't need you. I don't need them. I'm doing just fine all by myself." This attitude of rigid self-sufficiency is a determined stance to not be hurt or rejected by another. Colleen, at age thirty-five, was extremely capable. While she allowed herself to get married, she didn't allow herself any interdependency. "I take responsibility for all of my needs. I always have. I never trusted that I would be heard, so I didn't share my desires, my wants. It wasn't that Gerry wouldn't have been there for me—I just didn't give him a chance. I was so used to not trusting that anyone would be there for me or follow through with their promises, it didn't dawn on me to ask others to be there. After all, I became an expert at taking care of myself."

Unfortunately, this dynamic became a major source of discord in Colleen's marriage. She and Gerry were not able to achieve the intimacy Gerry wanted and he ultimately chose to leave the marriage. Colleen stayed out of any committed relationships for the next twelve years. Looking at her issues of trust, fear of rejection, and fear of asking others to be there for her needs is her focus in recovery today. It is Colleen's hope that she will allow herself the intimacy she deserves.

Identifying Now What You Needed as a Child

To become more skilled at recognizing your needs as an adult, you have to be empathetic to your childhood needs. Because your needs today are often the same as when you were a child, discounting your past needs only serves to detract from believing that you have a right to meet your needs as an adult. In working with clients, I have found that for adults to identify their unmet needs as children, it is very helpful for them to go through an exercise of writing a letter to their parents. This exercise also leads them to see that those childhood needs are often their needs today. This letter will never be mailed, read to, or given to that parent. The purpose is not to retaliate, blame, or hurt the parent. The purpose is to facilitate the grief process and identify needs.

Here is an example. It is a letter written by a thirty-three-year-old woman.

Dear Dad,

I want to thank you for some things when I was young. I am glad you told me you loved me. I believed it. I always liked it when we played. But Dad, there was so much I needed that I just didn't get. You became so tyrannical, so controlling, and so dishonest. More than anything, I needed you to let me be a kid, to let me make mistakes. I lived in fear of not being perfect for you. By being perfect in your image, I gave up my childhood. I needed to play, Dad. I needed to be me and not just a part of your self-image.

I needed you to be nicer to Mom. You never remembered her birthday, or bought her a Christmas present. Because you drank, she was always at work. I needed to know her better. As a teenager, I hated the fact I was so fearful of you. I was scared, terrified all the time. I hated how I felt sexually. I felt so dirty because of your attitude about boys and me. I always felt ashamed. The funny part, Dad, is I wasn't sexually active. I needed to eat dinner as a family. We ate anywhere from 7:30 at night until 11:30. There was nothing ever pleasant about dinner. You didn't even eat half the time. You know what, Dad—I still need you.

This letter elicits many powerful feelings. This is the kind of letter that helps to move you through the grief process and at the same time helps you become empathetic to your own plight as a child. It also allows you to see how your childhood needs are often carried into adulthood. In the above letter, this woman identified her childhood needs as:

1. I needed to be a kid.
2. I needed to play.
3. I needed to make mistakes.
4. I needed to be me, not you.
5. I needed to know Mom better.
6. I needed to feel comfortable with my sexuality.
7. I needed healthy rituals.

8.   I needed you, Dad.

By identifying these childhood needs, the writer identifies her present day needs. These aren't needs that her parent will meet today, but they are still present-day needs, irrespective of age. An exercise like this says:

1.   I need to play, to discover my spontaneity, frivolity, creativity.

2.   I need to feel I am of value even though I make mistakes.

3.   I need to discover who I am separate from my father's needs of me.

4.   I need to know my mother better.

5.   I need to feel comfortable with my sexuality.

6.   I need healthy rituals.

7.   I need my father.

This woman at thirty-three, or at any age, can still work on these needs. Of course, her parents may not be available or accessible, but owning the need is the first step to coming to terms with it.

SETTING LIMITS AND BOUNDARIES

Beginning to meet your needs leads you to the next recovery skill, which is setting limits and boundaries. Being raised in troubled families meant that our boundaries as children were not respected, often not even recognized. Or we may have lived with rigid, walled boundaries, offering no opportunity for any emotional or spiritual connection. Unhealthy boundaries create confusion about who is responsible for what, adding to more distortion about guilt and shame. As a result of living with chronic boundary violation/distortion, we are often either not skilled in setting boundaries or we are disrespectful and intrusive of others' boundaries.

A boundary is a limit or edge that defines you as separate from others— a separate human being, not someone else's possession. For each of us, our skin marks the limit of our physical self. We have other boundaries as well. We have limits to what is psychologically and physically safe. We have emotional, spiritual, sexual, relationship, and intellectual boundaries. Emotional boundaries define the self, our ideas, feelings and values. We set emotional boundaries by choosing how we let people treat us. Our spiritual development comes from our inner self. Only we know the spiritual path for ourselves. We have sexual boundaries, limits on what is safe and appropriate sexual behavior. We have a choice about whom we interact with sexually and the extent of that interaction. We have relationship boundaries.

The roles we play define the limits of appropriate interaction with others. Our intellectual boundaries offer us the opportunity to enjoy learning and teaching. They allow us to be curious and inspired. Because we were raised with unhealthy boundaries, we often normalize hurtful behavior and can't recognize boundary distortion. The following are various types of boundary violation.

Emotional:
- ✓ feelings denied
- ✓ told what we can and cannot feel
- ✓ being raged at
- ✓ being criticized
- ✓ being belittled
- ✓ lack of expectations
- ✓ being terrorized

Spiritual:
- ✓ going against personal values or rights to please others
- ✓ taught to believe in a hurtful Higher Power
- ✓ no spiritual guidance
- ✓ no sense of prayer or gratitude

Sexual:
- ✓ being sexual for partner, not self
- ✓ lack of sexual information during puberty
- ✓ given misinformation about our bodies, our development
- ✓ shame for being wrong sex
- ✓ exposure to pornography
- ✓ sexualized comments
- ✓ all forms of sexual abuse

Relationship:
- ✓ falling in love with anyone who reaches out
- ✓ allowing someone to take as much as they can from you
- ✓ letting others define your reality
- ✓ believing others can anticipate your needs

Intellectual:
- ✓ denied information
- ✓ not allowed to make mistakes
- ✓ not encouraged to question
- ✓ being called stupid
- ✓ encouraged to follow a parent's dream rather than your own

Physical:
- ✓ accepting touch you do not want

- ✓ not taught appropriate hygiene
- ✓ violence, pushing, shoving, kicking, pinching, excessive tickling
- ✓ hitting
- ✓ touch deprivation

Boundaries are the mechanisms that bring safety into our lives by establishing healthy control. Boundaries are statements about what we will and will not do. Boundaries act as limits for what others can and cannot do to us. By setting boundaries for ourselves, we are exercising our inherent power to declare that we are autonomous individuals in our own right, not possessions or extensions of anyone else.

As a child, you had little power to determine your interactions with the world. You had no way to defend against boundary invasions. Yet, being invaded—used, abused, or violated—you believed you had no personal worth, having been treated as an object or possession, not a person. You may have believed you were bad or weak because you couldn't stand up for yourself. Today, as an adult, you can develop and strengthen boundaries, giving you a source of inner strength. Before we can establish healthy boundaries it is helpful to the process to identify boundary violations in your life. Think about significant people in your growing up years and reflect on the six areas of boundaries with each person. Note the healthy boundaries and unhealthy boundaries that were experienced.

Repeat this same exercise with the significant people in your life today.

Once identified, you are in a better position to redefine them for a healthier self. Healthy boundaries are flexible enough that we can choose what to let in and what to keep out. We cannot maintain boundaries without the ability to know our feelings. Feelings are our signals to comfort, safety, discomfort, danger.

We want to have boundaries that are flexible but with limits; they move appropriately in response to situations—out for strangers, in for those we are intimate with. They should be distinct enough to preserve our individual self, yet open to new ideas. They are firm to maintain values and priorities, open to communicate our priorities. Boundaries tell us that certain behaviors are inappropriate in the context of certain relationships. A healthy boundary protects without isolating, contains without imprisoning. Our ability to protect ourselves psychologically and physically is related to the strength of our boundaries. Boundaries bring order to our lives. As we strengthen our boundaries we gain a clearer sense of ourselves and our relationship with others. They empower us to determine how we'll be treated by others.

Establishing healthy boundaries is vital to recovery, to getting needs met, to developing a sense of self. All of this leads to being strong enough to be able to separate yourself from past shameful messages and behaviors—and to no longer internalize shame. Developing boundaries is knowing your physical and psychological comfort zone—a safety zone—knowing what you like and don't like. It is having a sense of your own self separate from others. It is a part of defining who you are. In recovery you need to ask yourself what it is you want. What do you need? What do you desire? One establishes boundaries that allow those wants to happen. Limit setting is the skill that allows one to maintain boundaries. In order to protect boundaries, in order for them to remain intact and useful, you need to know your feelings. Feelings are cues and signals to whether those boundaries are being respected. As well, one must believe their needs are important to be able to define boundaries.

Fear of rejection, the need for approval, and fear of anger are major stumbling blocks to defining boundaries and a willingness to set limits. If you believe you have done the work you need to do to be better skilled in establishing boundaries, but are nonetheless stuck, go back and address these three stumbling blocks. The skills to be able to set limits and establish boundaries take you to another issue and that is the ability to say no and yes. By establishing boundaries and setting limits, we begin to use the words no and yes with freedom. For so many of us, it was not safe to say no as a child. Without the freedom to say no, yes was said with tremendous fear and helplessness or out of a desperate need for approval and love. Others of us grew up in families where no meant yes and today we cannot hear when people say no.

There is often pain and confusion around how no and yes were offered in troubled families. That pain needs to be acknowledged. As with the other foundation issues, you will need to apply the four steps to no and yes in your life.

A part of recovery will mean talking about the many times you couldn't say no but wanted to (all the times you said yes out of fear), and the anger and the pain that goes with that. You need to acknowledge the times you heard yes when you needed to hear no. In recovery you will recognize that no can be a word that acts as a friend to protect you. It offers you choice. In doing so it will allow you to be more sensitive to others' boundaries. We all have the power and right to say no and yes. It is my hope that yes is a right that is offered freely rather than out of fear or the need for approval, and that when we say no we are actually saying yes to ourselves. Here is an example of the four recovery steps applied to setting limits and establishing boundaries.

Step One: Describe both the healthy and unhealthy boundaries you experienced in your growing up years. Be willing to feel the pain associated to those experiences.

Step Two: Describe how those childhood experiences have an impact on you today.

Step Three: Identify specific beliefs you have internalized about setting limits and establishing boundaries. Are these beliefs hurtful or helpful to you today? Identify the ones you want to let go of and those you would like to maintain.

Step Four: Name specific boundaries that you would like to either strengthen or lessen. List them in the order of which is the most safe (easiest) to the more difficult ones. Begin with those that are safest. Congratulate yourself with each accomplishment!

Creating a Core of Strength with the Recovery Skills

The core recovery skills—validation, giving up control, feeling feelings, identifying needs, setting limits, and establishing boundaries—are the skills that will allow you to move forward with growing confidence. They are the skills that will offer you a foundation to go further in recovery and address more complex issues of loss, abandonment, and shame. You will be developing a true inner sense of self that will allow you to discover new choices and bring meaning into life. You will no longer just be a reactor; instead you will act on your own beliefs and decisions. You will no longer be propelled by fear or shame, but you will have a more solid belief in what you value, what you want, and a much more gracious, supportive, and forgiving attitude toward yourself.

Life will no longer be viewed through a lens of fear or doubt. You will rightfully expect more from life and feel hopeful. The foundation has been laid for you to continue addressing those areas important to you.

We would all like to avoid going through emotional pain—I know I certainly would. But we need to own and feel that which has been harbored in our body and soul so we can set it free. And, as we will soon discuss, our fear of feelings is often more powerful than anything that actually occurs when we feel. Know that you never again have to walk through the pain as a child and that you never again have to walk through the pain alone. While you would like to reach recovery alone, recognize that you have lived a life of isolation. So, wanting to go through this process alone often reflects the rigid self-reliance you learned, as well as not having learned to trust. You deserve to have help by allowing others to be a part of your process. There are many who will understand your emotional struggles and pain. Whether you choose to begin your recovery with a therapist, a Twelve Step group, or in treatment, there are literally millions of others who understand your resistances because they have struggled, too.

The awarenesses that have brought you to your turning point are much like a sailboat changing course. The boat simply "comes about," turns to a new direction, and the wind refills the sails. As you change course, the steps you now know, along with the skills you are learning, will harness or guide the power of the wind to help you move along your newly chosen way.

- You deserve to begin rebuilding your life in a new direction.
- Learning to love yourself does not mean you love others less.

Instead, it frees you to love them more.

CHAPTER 4

THE HOUSE WE LIVED IN

"What if we thought of the family less as the determining influence by which we are formed and more the raw material from which you make a life." —Thomas Moore, Care of the Soul

"When our worth and our identity are no longer defined by a survival role, we have choices about meeting our own needs and developing in our own ways that we did not have before." —Claudia Black

A family is like a house with many rooms. Picture the family you grew up in as one room in the framework of this very large house. The family you have now, as an adult, is the central living area; in fact, the "family room." Each of the other, different rooms of the house represents the previous generations of families and newly created ones, all of which are connected directly or indirectly. Through the doors to those rooms pass family secrets, family stories, and beliefs about what is and isn't true, and what a person should and shouldn't do.

FAMILY SECRETS

As we attend to our childhood issues, as we lessen our denial, we discover our true selves, and we may uncover family secrets. This is very frightening to family members who have spent years protecting themselves, and possibly others, from the pain of the truth. Recovery means letting go of the secrets. Secrets are handed down from one generation to another. Secrets are pieces of information that are withheld from others often out of shame, and many times with the intent to protect someone, be it yourself or another.

After his mother died, Kevin discovered a secret she had kept. Her parents had been from Austria, not Switzerland, as he had been told. Because of fear of religious persecution, they had changed their name and even the facts about who they were and where they had been born.

In Merle's case, her mother consciously chose not to tell her that she might pass on a physically disabling terminal illness to any male children. Afraid that no man would want to marry Merle, her mother thought if her daughter never knew, she would not be limited in her marriage options. In time, Merle had many suitors and did marry, but she also bore a child who died young from this trans generational illness. The mother's concerns were sincere and out of love, but in trying to protect her daughter as she did, she denied Merle the chance to make important decisions for herself.

As is often the case, the intent of the secret was to protect. While both Kevin and Merle understood their parents' concerns, Kevin was not able to share a piece of history and this created pain for him. He didn't have the opportunity to assist in lessening his mother's shame as he would have liked. He lost an opportunity for a significant intimate passage. As a result of her lack of information, Merle would experience the consequences of a decision her parents made for her, a decision that undermined the possibility of choice.

The Power of Secrets

Secrets are powerful because they can control you. Very often, the problem with a secret is not the content of the secret itself, but what you must do to keep the secret information out of sight. In a family, it is the proverbial skeleton in the closet and everyone in the family is held responsible to remain on guard in case someone outside the family gets too near the closet door. Whether secrets are passed down unbeknown to others or people actively collude to hide the information, it is fair to say that as a young child you had no choice in the matter; you were more or less coerced to keep the family secret. As an adult, you are now enforcing that secrecy on yourself. You may not be aware of it but you are the one making the choice to keep certain information away from prying eyes. The secret is just that—only information—and the choice is yours to tell it, to admit it, or to keep it hidden.

By admitting the reality of what is, you deflate the power of the secret. You can't drink away, exercise away, eat away, work away, or by any other effort rationalize away the power of the secret. The only way is to end denial, to admit, to open the closet door—that is the only way to get free.

Living in the Shadow

Being raised in a shame-based family means being raised in a family where there is a pervasive need to deny that family secrets exist. The content of the secrets may be especially fearful, seem especially awful, or the adult secret-keepers may be particularly rigid about the need to keep up appearances. Whatever the reason, all family life goes on as if under a dark cloud, because denial blocks the light of truth and shame grows rampant in the shadow.

Kevin's and Merle's mothers were the self-appointed, lonely guardians of the family secret, but some of us were raised in families where secrets were blatantly shared. In Lawrence's case, he reflects, "My dad had to go to the psychiatric hospital periodically. He was manic depressive. We know that now, but we didn't know it when I was a child. Each time he went, all of us kids were told not to tell anyone. If someone asked where he had gone, we were supposed to say he had to go back East to see a sick relative."

Cyndy remembers that "my older sister became pregnant twice, and each time we made up a lie for where she went for the last few months of her pregnancy. As soon as the lie was created, we were never to talk about her being 'gone' again."

These are secrets that the family members actively collude in. Yet, many of us live with secrets we don't even recognize. We may have lived with the secrecy of alcoholism without knowing it for what it was. Robin said, "I thought my dad was just crazy. He was forever a different personality. I knew he drank a lot, but so did lots of other people we knew. I didn't know he was addicted."

When we keep secrets we become adept at rationalizing and tolerating inappropriate behavior. As Gerald said, "I thought I came from a normal family. But it was only after three years of being sober that I started to take a look at most things in my life. I began to see that it's not normal for parents to make their children drink from a toilet because they are caught playing in it. It is not normal for parents to create 'beating circles' with their children to discover which one did something wrong."

In circumstances like Gerald's, there was no overt attempt to maintain secrets. Instead, there was a climate of secrecy about what occurred within the family. Pain was inflicted on purpose, but the children knew nothing different; the family was their only experience. Common to so many shame based families is the phenomenon of not knowing what "normal" is because everyone learns to tolerate inappropriate behavior. With the Don't Talk rule strongly intact and no other role models due to the family's isolation, all the family members are subject to ongoing hurtful behavior.

When we experience something in life that we don't have the language for, we literally can't talk about it, so the experience remains a secret. For example, some children don't identify their being abused because they are taught that physical abuse means being punched or slapped. They don't recognize that having their hair pulled is abusive. They don't recognize that being slammed up against the wall is abuse. Also, they may believe a certain behavior has to happen every day, so when it only happens once a month, they rationalize it and it remains a secret.

Any time we do not have support within the family for our feelings, we learn to deny the pain and to create defenses that protect our vulnerable self. In time, we normalize painful experiences. "It only happened once." Or, "He didn't mean it." There is a need to deny and to protect ourselves when we don't have the external protection from other family members that we need in order to survive. When that happens, we end up keeping secrets and not even recognizing the secrets are there. For some people the word secret implies an accompanying negative judgment. They believe that if the secret were known, they would be judged as damaged goods, as "less than" or "not as good as" others. Naturally, it is difficult for people with this belief to open up and admit their reality.

How can you tell if you are living with a secret? One way is to ask your- self, "Is there something about me or about my family that causes me to fear, if the truth were known to others? Would I be rejected as their lover, friend, or employee?" Another way of asking is, "Is there something I cannot tell anyone because I am afraid of a negative reaction? "When you feel an implied threat associated with divulging some certain knowledge, this is information that restricts your life.

The Origins of Secrets

What secrets did you grow up with? Were these secrets you were aware of at the time, or secrets you suspected and then confirmed later? Secrets are often about embarrassing illnesses or problems with the law, such as being convicted of a crime or being in prison. Other problems occur in situations where family members have had extramarital affairs, pregnancies outside of marriage, abortions, addictions, or are involved in physical or sexual abuse.

What secrets do you have as an individual? There may even be some things only you know. Randall said he stole as a child and even now steals little things from friends and family. As far as he knows, no one knows that.

Jeanne said she was raped and no one else ever knew. Many women who have been raped have kept that experience and all of the many associated feelings a secret. Delores kept the knowledge of an unwanted pregnancy and miscarriage from her own husband. Some of us have secret fears, such as, "What if I lose my mind like my mother did?" Other fears might be, "I'm afraid my marriage is about to end" or "I am questioning my sexual orientation." As we keep our secrets and carry the burden of hiding the information, feelings of guilt often intensify and fear of discovery escalates. Fear causes pain, and too much pain often pushes us into seeking some self destructive means of temporary pain relief. People keeping the secret of being sexually abused are commonly known to medicate their pain with alcohol, pills, or other drugs. Many people isolate themselves socially so they don't have to spend energy focused on what they "can't say." It is common to see someone in addiction recovery have a relapse when he or she feels extreme guilt for a secret, or even from the fear of discovery of a secret. When we carry secrets, our view of the world is distorted. We are forever in a defensive position with others because we are always on the alert to protect our privacy. Trying to somehow distance ourselves from this "hidden information," we rationalize, distort, and repress the information in a way that blocks us from opportunities for emotional growth and intimacy.

Phyllis, for example, didn't want her new boyfriend to get close to her family because she didn't want him to know certain things about them, such as her mother's addiction to pills or her brother's chronic abuse of cocaine. As a result, she would spend energy trying to stay separated from a significant part of her life. By not sharing the history of being sexually abused, Marie maintained a barrier between her partner and herself that directly contributed to the sexual difficulties they were having as a couple. When we have lived a life of secrecy, after awhile it just no longer occurs to us to share with and confide in others. When we haven't talked about something for five, ten, or even thirty years, it doesn't occur to us to talk about it today. We have had years of training in being closed, protective, and secretive. So when things occur in the present that create fear, guilt, or shame, it is even less likely that we would choose to share. And the longer we hold in those old experiences, the more our shame is fueled and the more we act it out.

Out of the Shadows, Out of the Shame

Recovery is living a life free from shame. It is recognizing that you are not your secret; you are not your family secrets. You are a person with a myriad of experiences, some of them very painful. But, the pain of exposing the secret very, very rarely compares to the pain of keeping the secret. And, once the shameful knowledge is shared, the relief feels like the warmth of the summer sun after a very long, cold winter.

The following are some of the reasons people reveal secrets:

1. It relieves a burden: You no longer have to continue to lie to others. The secret has made life more difficult. It is no longer necessary to spend any more energy keeping it. Tony found that he felt great relief when he told his parents, twelve years after the fact, that he was the one, not his brother, who was driving the car when they had the wreck where another passenger was seriously injured.

2. It allows you to be true to yourself: It allows you to be honest with yourself. By telling the truth, Tony didn't have to suffer guilt every time he lied about his car wreck. When he could answer, "I was the driver," he could validate himself for having the courage to admit he had made a serious mistake.

3. It prevents a possible surprise discovery: Some secrets are shared to lessen the shock or surprise that would be created if a significant other inadvertently found out. In fourteen years of marriage, Michael had not told his wife he had fathered a child sixteen years earlier. After this long time, Michael found tremendous relief believing that, even though it might be painful for his wife to learn he had a daughter and that he had kept the knowledge hidden all these years, it would be better for her to know now. He had decided that was a better option instead of some future day when the daughter might appear on their doorstep.

4. It enables you to have a more honest relationship with another: When you share a secret with someone, you are conveying the added message that you trust them with something very important to you. You are sharing at a more vulnerable level and that often creates in the other person a reciprocal willingness to be open and vulnerable. The result is that a greater trust develops between the two of you.

5. It stimulates family change: When you decide to speak up, other family members are encouraged to make changes in their own lives. By telling your brothers and sisters that your mother has a drinking problem (that all of you have been witness to but have ignored), you are taking the first step in breaking everyone's denial. Potentially, this could result in everyone receiving help, including your mother. By telling of your sexual abuse, you may set an example that will inspire other family members who have been abused to speak up.

6. It could be a plea for help: When the secret you confide still needs to be attended to (for example, if you are drinking too much and not yet in recovery), telling another person is a way for you to begin to move yourself toward getting help. If you were raped, telling someone, even many years later, may be your cry for help that will allow you to process unresolved grief and rage.

Secrets Become Confidences Shared with Safe People

As you create new ways of relating to the people in your family, it will be important for you not to play a part in the secrecy they may still want to maintain. Recovery does not include secrecy. It means speaking your truth. You must end the Don't Talk rule for yourself. However, putting an end to secrecy does not mean that all things are to be shared with all people. Some events are very personal, and you will not want to share them with just anybody. As you choose safe places and safe people to share with, the word secret dissipates, and the word confidence replaces it. As you consider with whom you want to share your secrets, you need to examine why you want to tell them. Sometimes people share secrets not to help themselves but to hurt others. Some people share a secret for the pure act of revenge. "You have hurt me, so I will hurt you with this! Did you know that Dad isn't your real father!?" Any time anyone considers telling some powerful and potentially hurtful information, it is necessary to look at the motivation. You could rationalize that the other person has the right to know. Yes, they do. But are you the one to tell them? Would it be more helpful to encourage a more appropriate person to share at a more appropriate time?

Not only do we need an understanding of why we are sharing, but also we need to discriminate with whom we share confidences. If you picture your family in that multigenerational home, know that you do not need to stand naked in front of your whole family. There is room for privacy. Curtains can be drawn around you, or you and certain others. By choosing safe people to share your confidential information with, you have developed an intact, flexible boundary. You choose when the curtain is drawn or closed, or whether or not the window blinds are pulled up or partially opened. The curtain of confidentiality replaces the rigid, cement-walled boundary of secrecy that blocked out all opportunity to create healthy relationships. In recovery you learn to develop boundaries and to trust your internal cues to know with whom and when to share.

When the whole truth is told about the past, because it has been previously discounted or even feared, it can be a real shock to the family system as a whole. As we begin to talk openly about what has happened around those experiences in the past, we may choose to do so gradually.

Telling a secret for the first time is a very powerful experience. We may feel great relief and exhilaration. The telling may tap a deep well of grief and pain. It is healthier for you to first share this information with someone you trust and know will be able to listen to what you have to say. Often this is a person who is not affected personally by the information. It may feel safer to share this information with a friend, a partner or spouse, another member of a support or self-help group, a counselor, therapist, or physician. Begin where it is safest. We benefit by hearing our words expressed out loud, allowing others the opportunity to offer us support and/or validation, either for our experiences and feelings or for what we need to do. The sharing of confidences lessens shame, relieves burdens and, in many cases, heightens intimacy.

Family Stories

When we address family secrets, we are also creating new family stories. But first, it is helpful to identify old stories. As you read previously, one of Merle's family stories was that you don't share potentially painful information with the affected person;

instead, you try to safeguard their options and make decisions for them. In her recovery, it is Merle's intent for the family story to be rewritten so her family today supports each other as they face difficult choices.

There is a new room that is yours for the making. You can decorate it any way you want; you can fill it with the best of your things. You have choices about whom you invite to come in. You can make decisions about how you act in your own room and in the other rooms that make up your extended family's home. Your own room, your own rules—a somewhat frightening, yet clearly exciting, opportunity.

IDENTIFYING FAMILY ROLES

Another significant change in the old homestead comes with the change of family roles. When you change how you interact with others in your family, you are changing your role. In the early years of understanding children from alcoholic families, it was extremely helpful for people to identify their own role in the context of their family. The concept of family roles became important because it offered a framework that helped affected families understand what was happening in their lives. This also made possible a language for them to talk about their experiences.

In addition, the newly discovered understanding of family roles offered validation to those who had an ability to "look good" on the outside, but who experienced great pain on the inside. The roles and the resulting restrictions helped people understand why it took so long for their pain to begin to show. Also, this was the first time the addicted family was addressed as a system. The labeling of roles has also been extremely helpful in addressing the problems of dysfunctional families whose issue was something other than addiction, such as mental illness.

By identifying our own role in the context of our families, we are able to recognize many of our strengths and vulnerabilities.

Roles We Have Played

As we address the ways we have been affected by families and begin to change the ways we relate to others as well as ourselves, we will find ourselves moving from a position of adhering to rigid role(s) to building from the strengths of each of them. Virtually everyone has strong survival instincts. As children, many of us needed those instincts to stay alive. When our environment was not a safe place, when it didn't have the structure, the order, or the predictability we needed, we did whatever was necessary to create safety. Those experiences became the basis for our survival roles. Each role offers intrinsic rewards to the individual person and to the family. Responsible Children, for example, bring order to the family chaos, facilitating for themselves and their siblings a predictable environment. In doing so, they personally feel a sense of greater control and often they experience external rewards. Adjusters play a more passive role, contributing to the family stability by being invisible, not having any expectations or demands, creating an emotional insulator around themselves. The Placaters take care of other family members' emotional needs, attempting to alleviate the family members' pain so the Placaters feel greater stability and then are also less aware of their own pain. Placaters are often liked for being so caring.

The Acting Out Children are attempting to be the voice for the family, saying "HELP!" or "Look at us!" Looking back, most adults see that they played not just one role, but a combination of roles. The majority of people identify with one predominant role and often operated within the other roles on certain occasions.

As an example, a person may identify most strongly with having been an Acting Out Child and, to a lesser degree, an Adjuster. Or one may have been both a Placater and the Responsible Child. For the person exploring his or her own roles, it is most helpful to look at each identified role separately from the others. It is easier to identify the strengths and deficits of each individual role, rather than two or more roles in any combination.

As people move into adulthood, they take with them the identity of their family role(s). A person who had been the Responsible Child will most often continue to demonstrate that role in adult relationships by being a leader and being goal-oriented. Mona, who was the Responsible Child in her family, maintained that position. She worked her way through law school, graduating with honors. By age thirty-one she was in private practice as an attorney. But, she was in private practice because she couldn't work as a team member. She needed to be in charge at all times. She had difficulty listening and was fearful of others who made decisions. By this time her third marriage was in trouble and she had no women friends. These were some of the consequences of strict adherence to her role.

People who identify with being the Adjuster still need someone else to provide structure for them to react. Steve was a man of many hopes and dreams but too frightened to make new decisions. He could adapt to any predicament and found his talent in working in large corporations. When they said jump, he did! Move—he did! Fire so-and-so, he did. He had three managers in three years. While other peers were upset, he thrived on change and unpredictability. Initially, his wife of three years liked that he seemed able to listen and that he was so "flexible," but now she demanded some things from him that were very scary. She wanted him to show conviction and initiative, to express his own thoughts. He was too malleable.

In one of his many geographic moves in the short time she was with him, she stayed behind and he moved on to a different city. The Placater, in adult life, continues to take care of people's emotional needs. Emily, at age thirty-two, was still the family referee. She had passed up two job promotions because, if she left the area, "Who would protect

Mom?"

While the strengths of these roles are so clear during the growing up years, it is in adulthood that the deficits of these roles begin to show. The Acting Out Children are the ones most apt to have experienced some form of direct intervention. These people are often in trouble with society in their young adulthood; they are thrust into systems, such as hospitals or jails. Either they stay a part of such systems or their role changes as a result of that system's intervention.

Because alcohol and drugs offer such a pervasive way for the Acting Out person to behave, many become addicted. At age forty-six Patty was still acting out her anger. In spite of having a college degree, her addiction got in the way of working in her field and she supported herself by bartending instead. Known for her belligerent attitude, she challenged nearly anyone who was in an authority position, from the local police officers to her bosses. As a result, few people welcomed her presence and Patty knew it. While Patty remains angry and addicted, many Acting Out people are sober and recovering today.

Not all Acting Out people become addicted. Depending on the depth of their anger and challenge of roles and authority, some have managed to redirect the strength of their skills and have mainstreamed into society.

Re-evaluating Our Roles

As much as we strive to create a healthier balance in our lives, we still struggle with what we want to keep and what we want to give up in terms of survivorship. After all, we never know when we may need to call upon those survival skills again. As you work on recovery, you will have the chance to see yourself in the roles you have played, and to identify the strengths and deficits that have been part of each one. Once you have done this, it becomes easier to recognize what harmful parts of those roles you need to let go of and what strengths you want to keep and develop.

Beliefs Give Strength to Our Roles

It is easy to see that many of the strengths found in our roles are to be valued. The problem is that they may have been learned in a context of fear, and so we still operate with fear as the basis of those behaviors. Or, they were learned in a vacuum; therefore, we didn't learn the value of the opposite perspective. We may have learned to lead, but not follow. Or, we practiced a strength to the extreme, such as being flexible to the point where we couldn't make a commitment to any one position. Individuals' experiences within their families are different due to many variables: birth order, ethnic origin, cultural values, economic circumstances, to give a few examples. These variables come into play when they are the source of our core beliefs. The beliefs we are taught, and those beliefs we pick up on our own, become the reasons our individual strengths become stronger, and eventually a rigidly repeated pattern of behavior, that is, an identifiable role. The behaviors are often fueled by our beliefs. The following are some examples of beliefs we hold that drive our behavior.

Beliefs of the Responsible Child:

✓ "If I don't do it, no one will."

✓ "If I don't do this, something bad will happen, or things will get worse."

Beliefs of the Adjuster Child:

✓ "If I don't get emotionally involved, I won't get hurt."

✓ "I can't make a difference anyway."

✓ "It is best to not draw attention to yourself."

Beliefs of the Placater Child:

✓ "If I am nice, people will like me."

✓ "If I focus on someone else, the focus won't be on me and that is good."

✓ "If I take care of you, you won't leave me or reject me."

Beliefs of the Acting Out Child:

✓ "If I scream loudly enough, someone may notice me."

✓ "Take what you want. No one is going to give you anything."

When you are in a painful family system, each of these positions provides some kind of reward. So, for example, the Responsible Child finds that life is more predictable and stable because he or she has taken charge of so much rather than to live with the chaos. This person garners esteem, as there are often societal rewards for good grades in school, a strong job performance, earning them a pat on the head by parents and community members. The Adjuster is not apt to be singled out for negative attention. The Adjuster is simply not noticed. The Placater is apt to be complimented and to draw positive attention. The Acting Out Child is rewarded with attention. (For many children, while negative behavior invites negative attention, that is often experienced as better than no attention.)

Transformation of Roles from Childhood to Adult Life

Our family roles have become the framework for our behaviors in all aspects of life. Our roles affect choices about careers, partners, friends, family, children, co-workers, and the way we feel about ourselves. These roles have framed our sense of identity. In recovery we ask, "Who am I, if I am not the role I have played all my life?"

"Who am I, if I am not the Placater?"

"Who am I, if I am not the Acting Out Child?"

"Who am I, if I am not the Responsible Child?"

"Who am I, if I am not the Adjuster?"

You are who you always have been—a good and valuable being. Your inner self remains creative, curious, hungry, wanting. Often expressions from that inner person were ignored, punished, or never developed. You no longer need your role as your survival shield, because you no longer need to take a protective stance against shame or fear. When our worth and our identity are no longer defined by a survival role, we have choices about meeting our own needs and developing in our own ways that we didn't have before. We don't necessarily develop a new personality, but we experience life without the need to defend against pain, and that means we are different in how we interact in the world. At the same time we let go of the shield, we honor that role because it served a wonderful purpose by helping us survive. Then the question arises, "What about the strengths I have received from my role(s)?"

Here are some of the specific questions people have:

"I am a nurse professionally. If I recover from caretaking everybody, does that mean I will have to change careers?"

"Anger is the only feeling I have ever known. Do I have to give it up?"

"My being so responsible and organized has made me a lot of money. I am a very successful businessperson. Will recovery take that away?"

"Flexibility is my name. Will I lose that quality if I look at these issues?"

Recovery does not mean that you are saying good-bye to the strengths of the role. While you want to keep the strengths, you can learn skills that create greater balance in your life. You can develop skills to replace the deficits of the role, and you can learn the skills of the other roles. Part of your new development comes with understanding why you act and react as you do. Another part is practice, revising your beliefs as you explore, questioning them, and gradually risking new behaviors that are congruent with what you really think and feel.

As you attend to the issues that cause you pain or restrict your personal freedom, you begin to develop a more rounded sense of self. You will not need the role to be the source of your worth, your identity. You will be defining your self from a broader perspective—a perspective of ascertaining your own values. You will be able to listen to your internal cues about what you need. You will have created belief systems that support a way of life you choose, versus a protective stance against shame or fear. And at the same time you can honor that the shield of your role helped you survive and so served a wonderful purpose.

Redirecting all of the energy put into trying to get your needs met by challenging the world will increase self-esteem, establish a connection to others, and create an ongoing, natural high.

Ending Old Roles

Just as recovery is a process, not an event, so is the task of identifying and re-evaluating the roles we have played. These roles are as old as our attempts to protect ourselves from pain. The resulting behaviors have become a matter of habit and the beliefs that have fueled them spring up almost automatically. Paradoxically, the roles do not bring us safety or freedom from pain. They restrict our lives in ways we can scarcely recognize and they are the present-day cause of much needless pain. Clearly, as Betty Ford said in her book on recovery, to free ourselves from these old ways is "a glad awakening." Rethinking our beliefs and reevaluating our behaviors sets us up to relate to our families, partners, children, friends, and to all aspects of our lives, in a much healthier manner. The task of recovering our unique selves, as we revise and renew our current ways of being, begins with awareness.

CHAPTER 5

THE FIVE STAGES OF ABANDONMENT

Through my own experience and in working with others, a conceptual truth has emerged. It is that for all of its pain and intensity, abandonment serves as a catalyst for profound personal growth. To explain this notion, I borrow the Japanese word akeru. Akeru is a word with many meanings, among them "to pierce, to end, to open." It helps to describe the hidden opportunity in abandonment. Shattering involves a painful transition from oneness with another to a state of sudden and involuntary separateness. You are left to experience the powerful forces that are at play as you strive to regain your balance. That a single word, akeru, embraces the concepts to end and to begin, helps us to recognize that there is a positive application for the energy created by shattering.

Shattering, in fact, is an explosion of separateness. Abandonment cuts us to the core, but a piercing awareness survives. The stabbing pain lets you know you are alive. The ego is cracked open, the defenses torn away. All that remains is raw sensation and the body's own urge to survive. Rather than try to submerge, deny, or ignore its discomfort, the task of the Akeru process is to go with it, take advantage of this raw sensation, and make it work for you.

Shattering creates an opening. Its throbbing lets you experience the very center of yourself as never before. You are finally feeling your yogic center, which allows you to bring healing energy directly to the source of your deepest wound. The secret is to get into the moment and stay there as often as possible. This helps you work with the energy rather than against it, to experience this time of stark, naked separateness for all that it's worth. In the moment, you experience the intensity of life as a separate human being, a tingling, throbbing speck of awareness in the universe.

Getting into the moment involves opening up your senses and focusing your attention upon the sights and sounds and smells and other sensations within your immediate environment. It means using your eyes and skin and ears to experience the moment in a very conscious way. Many call this mindfulness. Others call it Zen. Abandonment recovery calls the moment a natural refuge from emotional pain, and a chance to create lasting changes.

When a relationship ends, it is painful for both people, but the pain is especially debilitating for the one left behind.

"In my case, it happened out of the blue," said Marie. "One night, Lonny didn't come home from work. When I didn't hear from him after only an hour, I started jumping to the worst conclusions—car accident, heart attack. Never mind how much worse these visions got when he still wasn't home six hours later. The last thing I imagined was that he was with someone else. Why would he want to be? We were lifelong companions and lovers, best friends, and happily married for over twenty years. "Finally, I heard his footsteps crunching along the gravel driveway. I ran to meet him at the door. 'What happened?' I asked. My heart was in my throat.

"There was a pause.

"'I'm not happy,' he said flatly.

"'Happy?'

"He vaguely said something about how things were different between us.

"'Different?' I asked.

"'Don't interrupt me,' he said. 'That's one of the problems. You always interrupt.'

"My face was suddenly hot and pulsating. This was not Lonny.

"Then he uttered the words that turned my stomach upside down and left my mouth dry.

"'I'm leaving,' he said.

"I stopped breathing. It was hard to collect a single coherent thought. The only logical explanation

I could come up with was that he must have had a head injury sometime during the day. Why would he say what he was saying? I thought briefly but seriously about calling an ambulance.

"When I finally managed to speak, my voice came out deep and hollow, like it belonged to someone else.

"'You don't really mean this,' was all I managed to say in my strange, unsteady new voice.

"'I'm leaving this weekend.'

"I leaned on the kitchen table for support and tried to catch my breath from the dagger thrust into my gut. 'Is there someone else?' I asked, my voice coming in a whisper.

"He flatly and angrily denied this. But a month after he actually moved out, I was to learn that in fact there was someone else—another teacher from his school. It lessened the bewilderment but not the wrenching pain.

"I spent the first few weeks alone, trying to grapple with the immensity of it all. This was a man I'd loved with all my heart and soul. He'd always been so tender, his goodness always shining right through. For me, loving him had almost been a religious experience. I'd had such reverence for how he lived his life. He was a kind and caring father, both wise and sensitive.

"At night, I'd attempt to put the agony to rest and go to bed. But sleep was out of the question. I would be tortured by the empty space next to me in the bed. How I loved to hold Lonny, my beautiful, sensual Lonny. I hugged my pillow instead, weeping, sometimes screaming into it, because the torment was so unbearable. I had every right to hate him for what he was doing, but all I could do was miss him and damn myself for letting this happen."

Abandonment's devastation can stem from many different circumstances, many different types of relationships. There are a variety of factors affecting the way we react to the loss: the nature and duration of our relationship, the intensity of the feelings, the circumstances of the breakup, and our previous history of losses. Being left by someone we love can open up old wounds, stirring up insecurities and doubts that had been part of our emotional baggage since childhood.

Almost all of us have experienced Marie's feelings. Someone has chosen not to be with us, not to "keep us." We feel suddenly cut off, alone, sent into emotional exile. Being alone isn't bad when it is something we choose for ourselves. When someone decides to leave us, it is a different story. Bewildered, confused, outraged, we feel as if we've been handed a life sentence to which we've been unjustly condemned by virtue of some invisible defect. We yearn and ache for someone who has abandoned us, as Marie does.

Abandonment is our first fear. It is a primal fear—a fear universal to the human experience. As infants we lay screaming in our cribs, terrified that when our mothers left the room they were never coming back. Abandonment is a fear that we will be left alone forever with no one to protect us, to see to our most urgent needs. For the infant, maintaining attachment to its primary caretaker is necessary for its survival.

Any threat or disruption to that relationship arouses this primal fear, a fear that is embedded in the hardware of our brains, a fear we carry into adulthood. When children experience feelings of disconnection, they do not have the defenses to fall back on that we as adults do. Their wounds may not heal but instead float beneath the surface of their lives right into adulthood. Emotional experience is more painful when it echoes an episode from the past; that's especially true when it comes to rejection and loss. The relationship that ended today may be the fulfillment of your worst nightmares from childhood. Grieving over that lost love opens a primal wound. Someone deciding to leave you awakens this primal fear, and out of it rises intense anger. You feel angry for having to feel so much fear and desperation. You feel frustrated with yourself for being powerless, for not being able to hold on to another's love. You feel utterly and helplessly defeated over the circumstances of losing that love. You fear you are not attachment-worthy.

In some cases your grief may not come from a recent breakup; sometimes it is rooted in the residual insecurity and fear stemming from long-lost loves that interfere with relationships you're struggling with today. You may still be with your partner, but you understand that he or she no longer loves you. Though physically present, you grieve the loss. It's a steady throb tinged with feelings of personal failure: "Why can't I make it work? Am I not lovable? Why can't I get him to love me?" In other cases, like Marie's, a partner leaves you for someone else, in which case your grief is complicated by feelings of betrayal and jealousy. Sometimes there is no one else; your mate left because he just stopped wanting to be with you, needed his space. Your grief becomes fraught with feelings of self-reproach, anxiety, and lack of closure. You wonder: Are you so very horrible that you deserve this punishment—that your partner would rather be alone?

Or your relationship may have simply fallen apart—perhaps you weren't ready, or you two just didn't seem to be able to make it work. Perhaps the relationship was so painful that initially you were relieved by the prospect of separation. Feelings of inadequacy came as an aftershock. In these cases, grieving may be complicated by a profound sense of personal disappointment. You may feel remorseful, uncertain about your future. Sometimes you were the one initiating the breakup because you felt abandoned during the relationship. Or the abandonment was sudden and unexpected, in which case shock and disbelief took over. You must first address the desperate pain and debilitating panic before you can begin to grieve. The grieving process is similar to bereavement over a death: Loss is loss. But abandonment grief has a particular life of its own, stemming from the circumstances that led up to it and from the feelings of rejection and inadequacy that often accompany it. It is because abandonment's knife cuts all the way through to the self that it is so painful. You lose not just your loved one but your core belief in yourself. You doubt that you are lovable and acceptable as a mate. These feelings can become deeply inscribed, creating an invisible wound that causes you to turn on yourself.

Sometimes people feel the loss of a loved one so deeply and question their own worth so profoundly that it is as if there's an invisible drain deep within that works insidiously to siphon off self-worth, like a slow, internal bleed. The paradox for these folks is that when they try to rebuild self-esteem by doing esteemable things, their deep wound is always draining it away. This drainage of ego strength is crucial to understanding and working through the abandonment cycle. In fact, it is hard for me to understand why its special type of grief had gone virtually unrecognized, unstudied, and untreated until this book. Mental health professionals generally interpret the feelings of abandonment as a symptom of depression or anxiety. But abandonment grief is a syndrome of its own. It is the way in which your fear and anger are turned against yourself that gives abandonment grief its particular character. The tendency toward self-attack and self-recrimination represents the midway point in the grieving process. But injury to self (or internalizing the rejection, as I call it) is interwoven into all of the stages of abandonment. It is a persistent, ongoing process that causes us to abandon ourselves over and over.

What Is An Abandonment Survivor?

Abandonment survivors are those who have experienced the anguish of lost love and have the courage to go on believing in life and in their own capacity for love. Some are celebrities who have told us their childhood stories; others never make a public disclosure. Some are therapists—probably the majority of therapists have their own abandonment histories. But most are everyday people. There is an abandonment survivor in just about everyone, though some may not acknowledge it. The insecurity, longing, and fear associated with the loss of love are universal.

People struggling with the abandonment syndrome are plagued by insecurity and self-sabotage, yet many manage to lead productive, even stellar, lives in spite of it. Others find the chronic insecurity too disabling to fully express their talents. Abandonment survivors are sensitive, caring, and primed for love. But membership to this venerable group is not restricted to those able to achieve success in their relationships. Many continue the struggle to resolve the old abandonment wounds that stand in the way of finding love. For all abandonment survivors—those who've found love and those still seeking it—the impact of losses past and present can be found in the fragments of unlived life, unreached potential, and unfulfilled dreams still waiting to be redeemed through the process of abandonment recovery.

What Is Abandonment Recovery?

Abandonment recovery involves a program of five exercises outlined in this book. I call the program Akeru. You take action to heal the underlying wound of abandonment from past and present losses. You gain new information, identify unfinished business from the past, and practice hands-on exercises for improving your life. Anyone can benefit from this process. Abandonment recovery provides a new language and approach compatible with twelve-step recovery programs. Its program is specifically designed to deal with unresolved abandonment—the underlying source of your addictions, compulsions, and distress. Abandonment recovery is based on the most recent information from brain science and years of clinical experience working with the victims of abandonment trauma. The program empowers you to overcome your primal abandonment and its aftermath of self defeating patterns—and to reach your goals for greater life and love. If you've been holding out for the right words or the ultimate insight that will finally free you, beware. The magic bullet is not in any book or program. It is within you. It is that untapped energy that you will learn to redirect. Abandonment recovery is easy, even pleasurable. You must do more than read this book. You must put its wisdom into practice.

What Is An Abandoner?

Abandoners come in every possible size, shape, shade, age, gender, and disposition. It is often difficult to tell who is or isn't capable of being emotionally responsible— who is worthy of trust, and who is an abandoner. What complicates the picture even more is that one person's abandoner might be another's lifelong partner. The circumstances surrounding relationships are so complex and variable that it is neither wise nor fair to make moral judgments, point fingers, or draw generalizations. Let it be said that many abandoners do not set out to intentionally hurt someone. Many are just human beings struggling to find the answers to life's difficult challenges along with everyone else. But there are some who are callous, leaving a trail of discarded lovers along heartbreak's Appian Way. And there are serial abandoners, those who get some reward from inflicting emotional pain on those who love them. For them, creating devastation is their way of demonstrating power.

Even those who are not motivated by this need might experience a heightened sense of self-importance when the one they leave behind seems so desperate to have them back. In the light of the other person's pain, these folks usually don't admit to an ego boost or feelings of triumph. Instead, they air more humble feelings, like the guilt they feel over having caused you pain. They are usually easily distracted from this guilt as they get caught up in their new lives and new loves with greater gusto than before.

Some abandoners are able to bypass these pangs of guilt by remaining oblivious to the effect they have on others. They're in a general state of denial about the devastation they've caused. This denial helps them maintain an image of themselves as decent, caring human beings. It often comes across as callousness and cruelty to the one who was left behind to pick up the pieces. Some abandoners insist they feel as badly as you do. But the difference is, they don't have all of those rejection stingers piercing deeply into their psyches like poison arrows. Other abandoners, however, unable to deny the pain they've caused, endure their own genuine grief and remorse, parallel to yours, over the failure of the relationship. Abandonment recovery is dedicated to all of those who struggle to sustain relationships, abandonees and abandoners alike. You are about to discover the benefits of working through the various stages of abandonment. As grief stricken as you may feel right now, the process will help you avoid the pitfalls of suppressing and avoiding the pain. Burying your feelings leaves them unresolved. Unless you face them, they continue to interfere from within, and you may find yourself caught up in self-defeating relationships that end in abandonment over and over again. Unresolved abandonment is the root of self-sabotage. The recovery process that I've come to call Akeru is designed to reverse this injury. It provides a program of five exercises described in this book. Abandonment recovery helps you gain something from the intense emotions you are feeling, so that you can turn one of life's most painful experiences into an opportunity to grow and change.

What follows is a bird's-eye view of the stages that will help you get started on your journey. Being able to see the stages as one process will, I hope, give you some insight on where you are, where you've been, and what to expect.

Shattering

In this devastating first stage, you are in shock, pain, and panic, suddenly bereft of life's worth and meaning. You try to keep the shards of yourself together, but in spite of all your efforts, your faith and trust have been shattered. The severing of this important emotional bond makes you feel (temporarily) that you can't live without your lost love. Suicidal feelings are normal to this period. They are caused by despair that is overwhelming but only temporary. Old feelings of helplessness and dependency intrude into your current emotional crisis. Akeru provides a pain management technique that will help you get through the most difficult periods as quickly as possible and gain strength from them, allowing you to enter a time of rebirth.

Withdrawal

Love withdrawal is just like heroin withdrawal, involving intense craving and agitation for the love you are missing. You ache, throb, and yearn for your loved one to return. Human beings are genetically heir to a powerful need for attachment;

severed relationships do not end your need to bond. In fact, losing your relationship tends to intensify the clingy, needy feelings. The emotional tear triggers a psychobiological process that can include wakefulness, weight loss, anxiety, and emotional and physical fatigue. Akeru will show you how to work with the bonding instinct that is responsible for the wrenching pain. You can redirect its energy toward making a significant new connection to yourself, which has ongoing healing benefits.

Internalizing

During this critical third stage of abandonment, your emotional wound becomes susceptible to infection, which can result in permanent scarring in the form of damage to your self-esteem. This is when you suppress your anger toward your lost partner and beat up on yourself instead. You tend to idealize your abandoner at your own expense. Any implicit or explicit criticism from your ex is taken to heart. You become preoccupied with regrets over the relationship, agonizing over what you should have done or what you could have done to prevent the loss. No matter how hard you try to fight back, your sense of self takes a beating. Akeru provides the tools to help you access internal energy and build a new whole new concept of self. The exercise is designed to open new windows in your awareness, allow you to make new decisions, and set new goals.

RAGE

Rage is not the first time you encounter anger in this process, but during the first three stages, your anger was victim rage, that useless flailing in space or stabbing your pillow to death. It is not until this fourth stage that your beleaguered sense of self, under siege from self-attack, is ready to stand up and fight back, to take on the challenge of the outside world. Only then is your rage of the self-empowering, healthy kind. Its aggression can help you rehabilitate your life. Rage provides the energy you need to defend your newly born sense of self and to ensure your continued survival. Some people have difficulty expressing anger and need help to avoid turning their anger inward into an agitated depression. Sometimes you are afraid to express anger toward your lost partner for fear of losing any more love than you already have. Instead, you take your anger out on those closest to you. You can have unrealistic expectations toward others at this time; you expect them to replace the love and nurturance you are so sorely missing. When they fall short, you explode. Fantasies of retaliation and revenge toward your abandoners are also common to this stage, but there are better alternatives. The old saying is true: The best revenge is success. Akeru uses the energy of anger to help you turn your abandonment experience into a triumph of personal growth.

Lifting

Because rage has helped direct the energy outward, it helps to lift you back into life. You begin to experience a levitation of spirit and intervals of peace and freedom. You feel stronger and wiser for the painful lessons you have learned. Life in all of its fullness begins to distract you. You let go of anger. Akeru provides the tools to help you enhance your capacity for newness and love. The first letters of each of the five stages spell SWIRL. The word swirl echoes the cyclonic, continuous, flowing nature of your grief. Like any natural life process, the five stages are circular rather than linear. They represent a single process that is overlapping and recurrent, a process that can take place within an hour, a day, a month, or a period of years—cycles within cycles. You swirl through them over and over, until the tornado begins to weaken, and you emerge a changed person.

Yes, there is life after abandonment—full, rich intense life—but you will have to work to get there. The guiding hand is there to help you get through the pain, learn from it, and experience a stronger connection to yourself. You will never be as conscious, as acutely alive, as you will once you have applied the principles in this program to your daily life.

STAGE ONE: SHATTERING

Shattering is a tear in the dense tissues of human attachment.

- ✓ It is a feeling of devastation, unbearable pain.
- ✓ It is a powerful neurobiological process.
- ✓ It is the birth trauma revisited. It is rebirth.
- ✓ It is the breaking up of the storm clouds, the clearing of new sky.
- ✓ It is an epiphany of insight, an awakening of the emotional core.

Shattering is a bottom—a transforming bottom—the same bottom from which people over the ages have found redemption.

All of our lives we have been over prepared for a shattering—for an event that is capable of ripping us away from what we hold most dear—attempting to ward off circumstances beyond our control. Most of our life energy is spent making ourselves safe so there won't be a shattering. Then, when it happens, it knocks the wind out of us. But once we catch our breath, we are in a position to rebuild our lives and not just to self-medicate with the illusion of security.

Shattering releases the primitive defenses that have become counterproductive, holding us back. The armor that was once protective becomes restrictive and uncomfortable. For the person no longer crippled, the casts must come off or they become a hindrance. Shattering is what we feel when a relationship first ends, but it can also be the aftershock of earlier experience, an eruption of old, forgotten feelings. These eruptions are often reported by people who have gone through twelve-step programs to fight addictions. They discover, most frequently in the second year of the program, that their addictive behavior served as a primitive defense. It takes that long for the old defenses to break away and for true rehabilitation to take place. Shattering is not a new phenomenon, but by isolating it, we can better deal with it. We must honor the power of the shattering and harness that power in a disciplined way to create a truly healing environment.

Roberta's Shattering

Roberta is a sensitive person, intelligent and versatile. She has a gifted sense of irony, which she displays with brilliant timing and subtlety. She has a serious side, too, and loves to intensely debate political issues. She has a mane of golden hair and large, pale green eyes. All of it helped her captivate Travis, a conductor of a city orchestra. Roberta's main drawback, as her friends would tell you, was her choice in men. Travis was no exception. He claimed possession of the artist's temperament. That was how he rationalized his domineering ways and need for control. He could be demanding at times, highly critical, and self centered.

Roberta had to exercise all of her diplomatic skill to keep their relationship on an even keel. She agreed she'd probably be making a mistake to marry him, which paradoxically was exactly what she found herself probing him about one night at dinner. "What do you think?" she'd asked, looking down at her plate. Travis hadn't responded right away. "I'm not ready for that," he finally said. "Roberta, you know I'm just trying to have fun, have a good time." He muttered an apology about how shallow that sounded, while Roberta's heart sank. Why did I have to bring that up? For the next month, Roberta tried to cajole Travis back into the hot and heavy relationship they'd had. But he had become gradually more and more absorbed in his career. He began limiting their time together to once a week and could be seduced into sex only with effort. Roberta sensed she was losing Travis. Her friends told her it was the best thing, but she couldn't bear to let go. She couldn't bear going back out in the world without him, hated the idea of being alone. I'm too old to be going through this, she told herself. She was thirty-five.

Then it happened. She saw him with another woman. Roberta walked up to them and hit Travis in the chest with her bag. They exchanged words, his last being, "But, Roberta, I was going to tell you. I just didn't know how." Roberta showed up for therapy, crying and blowing her nose into tissue after tissue. "I never believed anything could be this painful," she said, holding her head in her hands. "It feels like my whole life is over."

Shattering is not unique to abandonment. It is the initial stage of all types of grief where significant loss is involved. But the shattering of abandonment is special. Your loss was not due to a death but because someone acted on free will not to be with you. In fact, if rejection, desertion, or betrayal played a part in your loss, it is not just your sense of security that has been shattered but your belief in yourself, your sense of self-worth.

"I feel like a complete failure," said Carlyle, his eyes swollen and bloodshot. He had lost nearly ten pounds in a little over two weeks and claimed not to have slept in days. "When I finally do fall asleep," he said, "I just wake up to the reality that it's over. And then my heart starts pounding, and all I can think of is to end it—just do away with myself. The only thing that stops me is my kids. "My wife wants me to leave by the end of the month. But how can I leave my family? They are what I've always worked for. They are my life. What have I done to deserve this? Why didn't I see it coming? I just can't face it all. I am too numb to know what to do about any of it—to know what I'm feeling. It's overwhelming."

Roberta and Carlyle are experiencing many of the "S" words common to this stage: the shattering of hopes and dreams, the sinking feelings, the sleeplessness, the soul-searching, the suicidal feelings, the shock. The important thing to bear in mind is that the intense feelings of shattering are temporary. In fact, shattering is the most short-lived of the five stages. Shattering is a necessary part of the healing process because it brings you to terms with the fact that your relationship is ending. The pain is wrenching because it represents a tear in dense tissues of an intense emotional bond. It is as if you have to be torn apart before you can rebuild a new self.

For most people shattering is a time of re-experiencing. Any old or lingering losses flood into your current wound. If you have been through a similar breakup, memories of that earlier loss come to the surface, forcing you to deal with not just your current loss but the whole issue of loss in your life. Your whole being is thrown into a kind of emotional time warp. Past, present, and future are thrown into the emotional turbulence. Shattering brings you in touch with feelings that may seem pathological when taken out of the context of grief. Freud, in one of his early monographs, Mourning and Melancholia, emphasized the difference between grieving and depressive illness. The intense emotions of shattering can sometimes even shake the clinician who hasn't come to appreciate the intensity of the abandonment experience.

Alby reported that his therapeutic relationship fell apart soon after his experience of shattering. The love of his life had just left him. Later, he went to his therapist's office and released his anguish in deep sobs. He reported feeling like a black tar ball long nestled within him finally broke up and melted away. His therapist, agitated by the display of the intense emotions, tried to refer him for medication. Alby had a stable job where he was highly regarded, was involved in creative arts and stable friendships, and showed no other signs of psychiatric distress. Ironically, Alby's ability to withstand the intensity of his feelings was a testament to his emotional health. As one abandonment workshop member put it, coming to Alby's defense, "Only the strong can endure the shattering; the weak need their defenses."

At first, people tend to swirl through all of the stages at once. You may go from the shock and devastation of shattering, to the withdrawal feelings of desperately needing a love fix and not being able to get it, to the shame and self-condemnation of the internalizing stage, to the burning anger of the rage stage, to moments of hope and clarity of the lifting stage, and then back again, over and over, one stage following another in rapid succession.

I have experienced every one of these feelings myself during different phases of my life: childhood, adolescence, and adulthood. My lifelong mate left me in the midst of what I had perceived to be a loving, successful, twenty-year relationship. His leaving was sudden, without warning. The irony that I had devoted my clinical practice of more than twenty years to treating abandonment survivors was not lost on me. Suddenly, all of those years of experience, research, and study were put to the ultimate test; I'd been abandoned.

Somehow, I had chosen to put all of my trust in a person who, after twenty years— after I had grown accustomed to a deep sense of security—suddenly one day said, "It's time for me to go." I found it hard to accept that I had been in the arms of someone who would abandon me after all of those years together. I knew that in my case, it was no random event, no mere coincidence. I knew that it had something to do with old losses, losses from as far back as my childhood. I would have to reach inside myself and find that last remaining seed, the hardy one that managed to lie dormant for nearly twenty years, and then spread its painful roots in my life again. I had to reach inside, find it, examine it, and uproot it once and for all. It was hard work, but it helped me to reach a new level of understanding and find a better path to recovery, not just for myself but for those who sought my help. True to my work with my clients, I faced my own abandonment honestly and openly.

My own breakup has taught me never to underestimate the intensity of another's experience but to listen closely and learn from it. Shattering is unique to each person. Its intensity cannot be measured by the length of a relationship. It is something that each of us finds our own way through. "But why must it be so painful?" some ask. "Where does the intensity of its pain come from?" I am going to take you on a journey through the shattering stage, exploring answers to that question. I will explain how losing a loved one activates the body's automatic system of self-defense and what this means in terms of stress. I will cover feelings common to this stage, such as suicidal thoughts, symbiotic feelings, shame, and the need for self-nurturance. I will help you identify unfinished business that may be amplifying what you feel right now, and describe childhood losses that may have stayed with you into adulthood. I will share relevant information from the field of brain science that will explain why memories of old losses reemerge during your current crisis, and how stress hormones can affect your childhood memories. I will define some of the characteristics of a syndrome that plagues many abandonment survivors—post-traumatic stress disorder of abandonment—and discuss the shock, disorientation, and numbness that are common to this disorder. The journey through the shattering stage will conclude with step-by-step instructions to help you to incorporate into your life the Akeru exercise for staying in the moment.

Shattering is a time of stark separateness and, although painful, offers the opportunity for tremendous personal awareness. At no other time are you better positioned to come to terms with your reality as a separate human being. This is why shattering, for many, becomes an epiphany, a portal to a whole new level of awareness, self-reliance, and connectedness.

THE ANATOMY OF SHATTERING

Sustaining The Heart Wound

During this critical first stage, people often feel they have truly sustained a heart wound. Shattering is when the wound is initially inflicted—the point at which you feel the knife that severs you from your heart's attachment. Your whole body reacts in protest. You may feel an aching or jabbing in your heart, a feeling of constriction, or a rush of anxiety across your chest. At first you may experience the frequent need to sigh or catch your breath. Your heart pounds when you come up against the reality of your loss. You may wake during the night in a cold sweat of panic and get up each day with a knot in your stomach. In fact, the stress of heartbreak and loss can trigger weakness of the heart muscle, a condition known as Takotsubo cardiomyopathy, also dubbed broken heart syndrome. Believe it or not, taking aspirin (and other heart medications) is known to help with heartbreak in some cases.

Your Self-Defense System Has Been Aroused

All of your physical reactions are the result of your sympathetic nervous system's response to your very real injury. Your body prepares you to fight, flee, or freeze in order to protect you from what it perceives as imminent danger. A rush of stress hormones flows through your body to keep your self defense system aroused, to sustain your alertness, to keep you on edge and in a state of action readiness. Adrenaline is released, heightening your brain's level of reactivity, supercharging your sensory apparatus to defend against the threat. It is no wonder that people refer to abandonment as a knife wound to the heart. Physiologically, your body reacts as if your heart had truly been stabbed.

Survival Instinct

Shattering indeed brings you in touch with the visceral forces of life. It exposes your core, arousing your most basic and urgent needs. Like childbirth, abandonment forces a separation; you're suddenly much more alone than you were before. It is possible that this experience is powerful enough to activate emotional memories stemming all the way back to your birth—bits and fragments of which have been encoded within the deep structure of your brain. The brain of a newborn does not yet have the fully developed structures it needs to record images of the actual events of birth. But the brain's emotional memory system is relatively intact at birth and lays down traces of early experience in the form of feelings and sensations. These feelings may be reactivated when an experience in your adult life bears an emotional resemblance to your birth.

For most of us, birth involved a sudden drop in temperature, glaring lights, noise, and perhaps a spank to get us to take our first breaths. When a loved one leaves you, a different kind of umbilical cord is cut. As when you were an infant, you've been suddenly disconnected from everything that gave you comfort, warmth, and sustenance. The infant calms when it is wrapped snugly—first in someone's arms and then in warm blankets; it reminds the infant of the warmth of the mother's womb. But what about you? You have been cut off as well. Are you in no less need of the comfort and human warmth you are suddenly missing? Some abandonment survivors in the throes of a shattering crisis report wrapping themselves in a blanket and even rocking themselves to and fro.

The tendency even for adults is to cry out for what is lost as if your very life depends upon it. For an adult, of course, this desperation is a feeling, not a fact. Your life does not depend upon your lost partner. It only feels that way. Shattering has indeed delivered you to a state of stark separateness. But who is there to receive you this time? Who remains to answer the urgent needs that have been activated? Only you. There is no nurse, no caretaker this time. Just you. You are just like the snail out of its protective shell, the cold and hungry infant. The recovery task for this stage is to take hold of yourself one moment at a time, to recognize that you are a separate person, a fully capable adult, responsible for your own self-care. It is no one else's responsibility to meet your emotional needs; only you can do that. Emotional self-reliance involves accepting the intense feelings of the experience, taking stock of your present reality, and assuring yourself that you will survive.

Split Thinking

Characteristic of the shattering stage is a feeling of hopelessness, an aspect of always-and-never thinking. Things will never be the same; you will always be alone; you will never be able to repair the damages; you will always be broken. The always-and-never thinking is part of a catastrophic mental process that represents a temporary return to the concrete either/or thinking patterns of your childhood. Shattering has temporarily thrown you into a time warp. Like a newly developing child, you have no real sense that you will live through this crisis and move on with your life's work or onto other loves. Instead, you are caught in a temporary double exposure. Your childhood perspective is superimposed over your adult self's more mature outlook, blurring your vision. You consequently see your current condition as a child would: ever-present, permanent. You may apply the same either/or thinking to the person who has left you, perceiving him or her as all good one minute and all bad the next. One moment they seem entirely irreplaceable, and the next you are saying, or at least trying to convince yourself, that you didn't need them anyway. On one hand you see your lost partners as completely justified for having left you; in fact, you have never respected them more or felt more awestruck by their fortitude of character now that they have dismissed you. On the other hand, you believe your partners have proven themselves to be morally corrupt cowards—that abandoning you was a dastardly deed.

This split thinking also applies to the way you view yourself. One minute you are a worthless failure for having lost the most important person in your life. The next you feel a sense of righteous indignation that someone would have the audacity to dismiss someone of your value. Maintaining a balanced perspective about yourself, your lost partners, and the healing process of life is difficult at this stage. Getting into the moment provides an immediate respite from the always-and-never perspective. When you are in the moment, this catastrophic thinking has no place. There is only now—a sacred place that you can create out of the bounty of life around you.

SYMBIOTIC FEELINGS

We have seen that during shattering we are flooded with feelings we knew best in our infancy, when we began as helpless, dependent children. The reawakening of these feelings has brought you in touch with the oldest, most long-forgotten part of yourself. In fact, the severing of your attachment has reactivated your emotional memories and has brought your most primitive feelings to the fore. Symbiotic feelings are the ones you experienced prenatally and during early infancy when you were in a state of oneness with your mother. You were inseparable, in fact, incapable of surviving without a caretaker. These feelings of dependency, triggered during the shattering stage, place abandonment survivors in a painful emotional paradox: The more you experience the impact of your loss, the more you are compelled to seek your lost partner. "I never wanted my wife so badly until she left," said Carlyle. "I felt I couldn't live without her!" Your friends and family may wonder how you could want someone so badly who has treated you poorly. What they don't understand is that your partner's leaving automatically aroused symbiotic feelings that had been stored deep in your emotional memory. You are left to cope with feelings that stem from psychobiological processes that operate independently of your conscious thought and beyond your immediate control.

It's common, for example, to become temporarily over reliant upon friends, family, and professionals for nurturance. Some people seek sympathy in ways uncharacteristic of them. Some develop unrealistic expectations toward others, driven by an internal craving for nurturance they can no longer find in their lost partner. Sometimes a mere perception of being slighted by a friend can cause them to overreact because it triggered symbiotic regression.

Michael's Shattering:

When Michael's lover first threatened to leave him six months earlier, he tried everything to hold on. He felt like he was fighting for his life. He'd made every possible accommodation to save his failing relationship, even gone into couples therapy and laid bare his emotional soul, but to no avail. One agonizing day, his lover packed up and left. Michael wanted to die. In spite of all the dread and anxiety leading up to the end, Michael had not begun to let go. In fact, faced with the specter of loss, he'd clung tighter than before. Now alone, he could not find the will to go on living.

A friend urged him to sign up for abandonment recovery workshops. He arrived unshaven and rumpled. Speaking in a monotone, he explained that he had taken a leave from his job so he could "crawl into a hole and stay drunk as much as possible."

He talked at length about his suicidal thoughts. At one point, the members interrupted.

"Do you really want to die?" they asked, "or do you just want the pain to go away?"

"I want the pain to go away," he answered listlessly. "I'm only happy when I'm asleep," he continued. "And I only fall asleep after I've drunk myself into a stupor."

"There are ways to manage that pain," we told him.

He waved that off. "It's too far gone for all of that," he said. "The fact is, except for the pain, I've already died. You can't save somebody who's already died." It is common for people to describe their abandonment as a kind of death. They report feeling dead, or wanting to be dead, or going through a spiritual death. As you follow Michael into the next chapter, you will see that it is important not to act upon these feelings. As intense as they are, they are temporary and will dissipate as you progress through the stages that follow. During the shattering stage, the hopelessness you are experiencing is a feeling, not a fact.

Many also experience their abandonment as a physical, even a mortal wound. They make frequent references to words that describe critical injury and destruction to vital organs, references to broken hearts, stabs in the gut, knife wounds to the heart.

"After Lonny left, my house had become a tomb, a torture chamber of loneliness. So I headed for anywhere but home," said Marie.

"On the highways, I didn't meet a stone wall I wouldn't have minded crashing into, head-on. If I spotted a knife while visiting a friend's house, especially something in a cleaver or butcher variety, I'd imagine plunging it deeply into my stomach.

"At night, I'd rummage through the liquor cabinet in search of something to guzzle down; it was the only way to fall asleep. The last thing I worried about at the time was becoming an alcoholic. I was more interested in inducing a stupor, coma, lobotomy, death—whatever could end the pain.

"I struggled to get myself together to go to work in the morning, and on the way in, I'd try not to follow my urge to drive off cliffs.

"It was a real effort to hold myself together for the classes I taught. It was hard coming up with new excuses every day for my bulbous red nose. I began to look more haggard by the day. People were always asking me what was wrong. Naturally, most of them were other teachers I didn't know well enough to tell about my problem.

"The good news about my deteriorating physical condition was that I lost weight, something I had always tried to do but couldn't because the truth is, I love food. Now I was more interested in the cutlery than the food. Friends saw me pushing my food around on my plate and asked if I was feeling well and why I looked so thin. My response was to thank them sincerely for the compliment and tell them I was on a special diet (called death wish).

"When I finally found out that Lonny had left me for another woman, I would have preferred that he just stick a knife in my heart. It would have been less painful, quicker, and saved me from nearly starving myself to death." We have already seen that during this critical period, many believe their devastation will be permanent. While this feeling persists, it is difficult to recognize that it is part of a process that leads to renewal. Like Michael and Marie, they truly feel their lives are over. The concept of death serves as an escape fantasy; it is the only way they can imagine an end to the pain. Conversations with them are riddled with references to death.

"I would be better off dead."

"I can't survive this."

"I can't sleep. I don't want to eat."

"My life is over."

"It feels like I'm going to die."

"Death would be easier."

Many abandonment survivors engage in fantasies about the impact their death might have upon their lost partners. "It would have been worth dying," said Marie, "just to get Lonny to realize that he really did love me."

For some, suicidal feelings, while not to be acted upon, can serve a purpose. They can help to shore up your ego during this stage. The idea that we could end the pain if we wanted to restores a sense of control that we have temporarily lost. But take pause. As powerful as your desire to end the pain is, these feelings are only part of the initial healing process. They will pass soon enough, and you will certainly find love again when you choose to. Your task is to get all of the support you need from the people closest to you, abandonment workshops, ongoing support groups, and mental health professionals. In the end, you will emerge from the experience better than before.

Somatic Sensations

You may not be able to pinpoint the bio physiological changes that are taking place under the surface of your conscious mind, but you may, after reading the next few pages, recognize some indicators of those changes. Your emotional brain perceives the loss of your partner as a threat to survival. The event triggers significant biological changes. As you progress through the rigors of your emotional crisis, many of the effects are sustained. Your heart rate and blood pressure are increased, sending a greater flow of blood and nutrients to the areas of your body needed for self-defense. Your digestion is turned off; blood flow is diverted from your stomach to major muscle groups so that you will be physically prepared to run away or fight off your attacker as the need arises. During the most stressful moments, structures deep within your brain signal a tightening in your vocal cords, creating the high-pitched voice of intense anxiety. According to Daniel Goleman, these same mechanisms make a dog snarl or a cat arch its back. Other neural circuits are signaled at certain critical times to put a fearful or angry expression on your face, to freeze movements in some of your muscles, or to cause your breathing to become shallow so that you will be better able to detect important sounds above the sound of your breathing. Other processes cause your respiration rate to increase oxygen supply to your brain so that your mind can sustain its state of hypervigilance and keep your attention riveted upon the emergency. Your bladder and colon prepare to void their contents to rid the body of dead weight so you will be able to move quickly. Your pupils dilate to let in more light; your vision is more acute. The cochlear cells in your ears require less stimulation; you can hear a twig snap off a branch hundreds of feet away. Your brain is unusually alert, even at night, as biochemical systems work to sustain what your body experiences as a lifesaving vigil.

Your neocortex continues to scan your memory banks, retrieving similar experiences from the past that it systematically sorts, compares, and analyzes to apply to your body's intensive problem-solving campaign. You experience this as obsessive thinking. Your immune system responds by lowering its production of antibodies, delaying swelling and pain to areas of your body that might become injured (in battle), so that your attention can remain focused on the threat at hand. You may not feel the impact of this lowering of your immune response until a few weeks later—perhaps during a respite from your intense emotional crisis. That's when you are likely to come down with that cold or flu.

Subjectively, you experience many of these symptoms in the form of constant preoccupation with your loss, hyper vigilance, a tendency to startle easily, gastrointestinal discomforts, and reminders of past hurts and old insecurities. You have trouble sleeping, relaxing, and eating. Alternately, you may be unable to stop eating, because your body is trying to shore up energy reserves for a sustained crisis.

The threat your body prepares you for is not an attack of vicious wolves or an earthquake but the loss of your primary attachment. There isn't, of course, a real, physical threat to your safety, but there is an intense internal battle going on. Many of these uncomfortable and unsettling sensations respond to the effects of a well-known drug— one that is legal and readily available—alcohol. Because alcohol is a depressant, it can dampen tensions and the edginess you feel. Even the most moderate drinkers tend to overmedicate with alcohol to help themselves fall asleep or relax. Since alcohol is highly addictive, it is important to remember that even in small doses it can impair functioning and lead to serious injury.

Try, as an alternative analgesic, to seek the refuge of the moment as described at the end of this chapter. Staying in the moment can help you feel centered and at peace, and it leads you to that state of calm that you need to get you through the most difficult moments, one at a time.

Shame

An issue that comes up for many people throughout the first stages of the abandonment cycle is shame. I'll discuss the shame of being left in depth in Chapter 4 when I explain internalizing. But when you first begin to grieve over a lost partner, you feel shame over emotional excesses you can't seem to control. "I can't face the world," said Michael. "All people have to do is look at me and see the condition I am in, and they'll know I'm unable to handle my life." We are socialized, men and women alike, to feel ashamed of intensely negative feelings. Many people hate losing control over their emotions, feeling helpless or in any way dependent. It's easy to overlook the valuable emotional wisdom contained in these feelings. But if you get in touch with them and understand what they are about, these feelings can enhance your future relationships. They allow you to become more emotionally accessible to others. Rather than accept and nurture these valuable feelings, many condemn themselves for being so desperate and needy. They allow the powerful feelings to throw their whole sense of personal strength and independence into question.

"I felt like a child," reports Richard, a bank president whose wife had recently left him. "I cried for her like a baby crying for its mother when she said she was going. My whole life suddenly revolved around her. I was obsessed with wanting to be with her, wanting to talk with her. I felt so needy and frightened. "I'm a grown man, but I wasn't able to tolerate being alone in my new apartment—it was too sterile, too empty. I was actually frightened of the pain I was in, afraid I wouldn't be able to live through it. It was shameful how dependent I felt. I couldn't help acting like a desperate child in the throes of a tantrum.

"I began to wonder if my whole adult identity was just a facade. I must, I reasoned, have been a weak, needy person all along. I even thought that it must have been why my wife left me in the first place."

Richard didn't realize it at the time, but the symbiotic needs he was feeling were temporary, normal to the process, and even served a purpose during the first stage of his grief. Until he was able to accept his needy and fearful feelings, he degraded himself, lost confidence. "I felt as if I had been utterly vanquished," he said, "like she was the stronger one." He was profoundly disappointed in himself for feeling so much pain.

There are several reasons to avoid feeling ashamed and simply accept your intense but temporary need for your lost attachment. First, as we have seen with Richard, shame only complicates the grieving process. It's one more way in which you turn against yourself. Second, when you attempt to disown, deny, or suppress feelings, you deny yourself the opportunity to better understand yourself emotionally. Third, burying your feelings delays resolving them within your current or future relationships. In short, picking up emotional baggage only prolongs your grief. If unaccepted and unresolved, feelings generate fear, anxiety, and insecurity when you next try to bring love into your life. Better to accept the cold, hard facts of the situation: that abandonment is a powerful enough trauma to arouse your body's self-defense system, to reactivate old emotional memories, and to create a temporary condition in which your need for attachment is uncomfortably intense. Coming to terms with the reality that losing your loved one is a real emotional crisis is a way to avoid the shame trap. This acceptance is an important step in the direction of becoming emotionally self-nurturing.

SHOCK

Not everyone is able to stay in touch with the most intense feelings of shattering. Some people report not being able to feel anything at all. "I don't know where I'm at. I'm too disoriented," reported Carlyle. Roberta says, "I know I'm in hell, but I'm numb. Everything around me has gone dead." Belinda describes her experience: "I flew to Paris to be with my fiancé, and when I got there, he told me he'd changed his mind. The engagement was off. I was fractured. Life in Paris, the city I'd always dreamed of, was going on around me, but I was too numb to see it, to hear it, to participate. Instead, I was in complete shock, standing alone with my whole life crashing down around me. Nothing seemed to matter. I wasn't even sure of who I was."

In their initial shock, people often appear detached from themselves and from the events going on around them. The extreme internal focus of this initial stage encapsulates them in a dissociative bubble through which the world can look distorted and far away. Shock is one of the many symptoms of traumatic stress, a significant component of the shattering stage. Some of its other symptoms will be outlined in the next section.

POST-TRAUMATIC STRESS DISORDER OF ABANDONMENT

Many people's reactions to abandonment share sufficient features with post-traumatic stress disorder (PTSD) to be considered a subtype of this diagnostic category. As with other types of post-trauma, post-traumatic stress disorder of abandonment can range from mild to severe. It is a psychobiological condition in which earlier separation traumas can interfere with current life. You experience emotional flashbacks that flood you with anxiety in response to triggers that you may not consciously perceive, and this often leaves you with the overwhelming sense that you're no longer in control.

John's Shattering

John arrived for his first session, a compelling figure, tall, good-looking, powerfully built. He had recently met a woman he felt attracted to. They had only one date. The evening felt right to him; he'd felt whole, complete in her company, and he wanted to make a real connection with her. He was sure she felt the same, but she didn't call him back.

"It was only one date!" he said. "I can't believe I am this distraught over one date!" He expected to be running into her at a professional conference that week and was afraid he'd be too emotional to handle seeing her again. "She'll think I'm a basket case. I won't be able to hide it. What could possibly make me overreact like this?" he said. "I'm obsessing every minute of the day. Not to mention the fact that I can't eat.

"It's not like I'm desperate for a woman or anything. I haven't even wanted to date anyone for a long time. And now I'm acting like this one woman not calling is a matter of life or death." He shrugged and looked to me for direction.

"Could it be unresolved grief over another relationship?" I offered. Point-blank, he confronted the pain that had been holed up inside. He took a deep breath and tried to speak. He made a couple of false starts—he couldn't seem to find his voice or control his facial muscles. Handing him a box of tissues seemed to help. His words and tears began to pour freely. The painful event happened about ten years ago. His fiancée had broken their engagement a week before the wedding. As he described this shattering experience, he seemed surprised that he could still feel the pain. "I thought I was completely over her," he said. "I haven't given it a moment's thought in years.

"After the breakup, I tried to date other people, but I just didn't feel right with anyone else. I was too insecure, too on guard. After a year or so of getting nowhere, I decided to go it alone for a while." This he accomplished by staying off the playing field, becoming a "devout bachelor," as he put it. The only side effect of his voluntary isolation was loneliness, but this was a steady throb, a dull ache he got used to. He considered it preferable to the ups and downs of romance. He told himself that there was nobody out there he was interested in, that he was fine by himself.

"So now I finally meet a woman I like, and I find out I'm a basket case," he said. "How could old stuff like this still have so much kick after all these years?" While not severe, John's case portrays one of the features of post-traumatic stress disorder of abandonment: intrusive anxiety from the past. His story focuses upon an earlier event from his adult life, one that continues to trigger fear and anxiety and interferes in his current life.

As John's case unfolded, he addressed childhood losses. When he was six, his father developed cancer and suffered a prolonged illness, forcing John's mother to work full time. Although his father's cancer eventually went into remission, the family business folded, and financial troubles forced them to move several times. There were numerous disappointments and broken connections for John along the way. John's childhood experiences made him especially sensitive to loss. As an adult, his strategy was to practice avoidance, to emotionally distance himself from his basic needs and feelings. He avoided relationships and the insecurities that went along with them.

There are many other patterns and behavior associated with a post-traumatic condition and many ways in which the fear or anxiety rising from your past separations may lead to emotional hijacking and may be interfering in your life today. A member of my workshop at the Esalen Institute testified to the heightened vulnerability she felt as a result of her childhood abandonment trauma.

"I become so vulnerable when I try to be in a relationship . . . It's like being a burn victim. The slightest breeze causes pain."

Signs And Symptoms Of Post-Traumatic Stress Disorder Of Abandonment

While not yet accepted into diagnostic literature, I propose the following list of symptoms for abandonment's post-trauma.

• An intense fear of abandonment (overwhelming insecurity) that tends to destabilize your primary relationships in adulthood

• A tendency to repeatedly subject yourself to people or experiences that lead to another loss and another trauma

• Intrusive reawakening of old losses

• Heightened memories of traumatic separations and other events

• Conversely, complete or partial memory blocks of earlier events

• Feelings of emotional detachment from past crises

• Conversely, difficulty letting go of the painful feelings of old rejections and losses, which generate ongoing emotional conflict with your parents or siblings

• Episodes of self-destructive behavior

• Difficulty withstanding the normal emotional ups and downs of an adult relationship

• Difficulty working through the normal levels of conflict and disappointment within a relationship

• Extreme sensitivity to rejection

• Tendency to emotionally or sexually shut down, but not be able to identify why

• Difficulty naming your feelings

• Difficulty feeling the affection and other physical comforts offered to you by a willing partner

• A pendulum swing between fear of engulfment and fear of annihilation

• A tendency to avoid close relationships altogether

• Conversely, a tendency to rush into relationships and clamp on too quickly

• Difficulty letting go because you have attached with emotional epoxy, even when your partner is unable to fulfill your needs

• An excessive need for control, whether you're controlling toward others or overly self-controlled; a need to have everything perfect and done your way

• Conversely, a tendency to create chaos by avoiding responsibility and procrastinating, and feeling out of control

• A tendency to have unrealistic expectations and heightened reactivity toward others, creating conflict that can lead to alienation1

• A tendency to act impulsively without being able to put the brakes on, even when you know there could be negative consequences

• A tendency toward unpredictable outbursts of anger

Not all of you who experienced traumatic losses during childhood were destined to develop these post-traumatic personality traits. Many psychobiological factors are involved in determining whether your earlier emotional traumas might lead to the development of a true clinical picture of post-traumatic stress disorder. Many people who suffer from post-trauma of abandonment aren't able to identify any extreme abandonments in childhood. Instead, they came from relatively intact families with no known history of abuse. On the other hand, there are those who endured extreme childhood losses and yet appear relatively trauma-free as adults—able to weather rejection and loss without signs of post-traumatic stress. The reason for this apparent discrepancy may have to do with genetic endowment and other predisposing physiological and psychological factors. Researchers have speculated that some people are born with a tendency to produce higher concentrations of norepinephrine, a brain chemical involved in arousal of your body's self-defense response. This would mean that your threshold for becoming aroused is lowered, and you are more likely to become anxious when you encounter stresses in life that are reminiscent of childhood fears and experiences, hence more prone to becoming post-traumatic.

Whether or not you are a candidate for a diagnosis of post-traumatic stress disorder of abandonment, you may be experiencing some emotional overlay from your earlier losses. If so, this re-experiencing tends to intensify your loss.

During the shattering stage, abandonment survivors experience many of the same symptoms as victims of other types of trauma, such as rape or physical attack. The difference is that abandonment survivors are not often recognized as such. Yet the shock, numbing, disorientation, outbursts of anger, and tendency toward risk-taking are all symptoms of significant trauma. The following testimonial comes from an abandonment survivor who reached out through my website. "I woke up every night missing her so intensely that my skin burned and I sweated for days at a time. A friend of mine who was a combat veteran said he had the same experience in Nam.

His skin would burn, his mind would race, and he could not stop sweating the entire time." We can see these symptoms in children who have been through abandonment experiences. Unlike adults, children do not have the tools with which to temper the impact. Their hurts and abandonments can leave a powerful imprint upon their developing brains and can affect their emotional responses throughout life.

The Shattered Personality Profile: Possible Precursors To Ptsd Of Abandonment

You may find that you struggle more during one stage of the abandonment process than another. Abandonment survivors who tend to have the most difficulty during the shattering stage are those who suffered devastating repetitive losses, personal disappointments, and upheavals in childhood. These might include the following:

- ✓ Death of a parent
- ✓ Physical abandonment by a parent
- ✓ Being in the middle of your parents' custody or divorce battle
- ✓ Prolonged emotional distance from your caretakers
- ✓ Physical or sexual abuse
- ✓ Being sent to a foster home
- ✓ Many of you may be the products of relatively intact families, but you experienced feelings of
- ✓ prolonged deprivation due to the following:
- ✓ Injustices within the sibling pecking order
- ✓ Chaos and conflict in family structure
- ✓ Emotional messages that left you in a double-bind situation where you couldn't win, no matter
- ✓ how you played it
- ✓ Rejection or exclusion from a peer group
- ✓ Prolonged childhood injury or illness
- ✓ Traumatic adolescent heartbreaks
- ✓ Significant disappointments (working hard toward something and failing to get the reward)

The shards and fragments of these and other traumas are reactivated when you go through similar upheavals and losses later in life. For many abandonment survivors, this means intermittent emotional turmoil and chronic uncertainty about yourself and your relationships. As new experiences trigger the old emotionally charged memories, your self-defense system kicks in, releasing adrenaline and other stress hormones. The process leaves many feeling on edge and suddenly uncomfortable in their own skins. When people who are prone to anxiety or those with traumatic childhood histories encounter a new crisis, the old shattering can be truly overwhelming. Without an understanding of what causes the intense anxiety or how to cope with it, some desperate folks self-medicate with drugs and alcohol. If you feel overwhelmed, please seek professional help. Support and guidance are available; in some cases, medication may be appropriate. It is not through any weakness on your part that you cannot by an act of conscious will rid yourself of the anxiety, pain, and fear. These intense emotions spring from the psychobiological nature of your crisis. Shattering is a time of trauma, but it can lead to a new level of self-acceptance and understanding of life if we choose to learn from its wisdom.

The Benefits Of Shattering

The secret gift of abandonment is that it has helped you find your way to old wounds from traumatic events you may not even recall. Finally you can address unresolved feelings. Shattering has accomplished what many psychoanalysts strive for in years of therapy—bringing you to the seat of your unconscious conflicts. You are in a crucial period during which you must look to your own resources. You can no longer look to your lost partners for security and nurturance. Beyond the support of friends, family, and helping professionals, you spend most of your time with yourself; you are in an optimal position to look inside for strength. Though your own parents may have tried, they were not able to sufficiently assuage all of your abandonment fears when you were children. As an adult, you face this challenge alone. First you must be in touch with your fears. Listen to what they are telling you about your emotional needs. Shattering has been a journey to the center of the self, preparing you for deep healing, for the opportunity to shape your life from the inside out. It challenges you with critical questions designed to help you find the point from which you can begin again.

- ✓ Can you accept your own separateness?
- ✓ Can you face the ever-changing world around you?
- ✓ Can you take responsibility to direct it?
- ✓ Can you acknowledge that you are capable of benefiting from your abandonment?
- ✓ Can you accept that you are able to stand on your own two feet?

Recognize that you have already gained something from your experience. The casts and crutches of your former life have been broken; the false ego has been crushed; you've awakened from a trance. You have been jolted out of complacency, thrown out of equilibrium, and forced to find a new way back. Carlyle put it this way:

"For me, shattering was an awakening. It helped me to change the direction of my life. I know I have a lot of work to do, but I finally know what's important. It took losing my wife to finally shatter my illusion of permanence, of being one with someone, of being in control. For the first time in my life, I realized how alone I was, how alone we all are.

"From somewhere in the abyss I was in, missing my kids and feeling lost, I was able to look up and be astounded at how painful loss is. Not just mine. All loss. I started to think about the millions of people who've suffered this experience before me and the millions to come. I was on intimate terms with human pain.

My touch plate of feeling was alive as never before. And I knew I was forever changed by this knowledge. Painful as this was, it was a gift I would never give away. It made me intensely human."

Shattering has laid down its challenge to you. Through it you can achieve greater emotional independence, an undertaking that may be long overdue. Being emotionally independent does not mean accepting that you are condemned to live your life alone, but that you are able to reach for love and connectedness with self-reliance and emotional wisdom.

RECOVERY FROM SHATTERING

Preparing Yourself for the Moment

Begin right where you are. Just stop whatever you are doing and take in your immediate surroundings. Is there natural light or lamplight? Is the room sparse or cluttered with many things? Take it all in: the sights, the sounds, the feeling of the room. Experience your own heartbeat, the rhythm of your breath. You're going to isolate one of these sensations and use it as a tool to gain entry into the moment.

Listening for Background Noises

Some people, wracked with the torment of shattering, respond most quickly to listening for background noises, trying to discern the farthest sound. Is it quiet where you are now? Or do you hear the blaring noise of a radio or television? If you can, turn them off. Your goal is to remove any sounds that can drown out subtle background noises. Listening for faint background noises requires all of your attention. The concerted effort creates a momentary oasis of pure experience. Close your eyes and focus your attention on the sounds you hear. At first, the loudest noises command your attention. You may hear someone's voice in the background or people moving around in other rooms or a truck driving by. Try to identify all of the sounds you hear. Now listen more closely. Can you hear the distant sounds of birds? Can you hear cars on faraway streets? Can you hear the hum of an appliance in another room—the refrigerator or a ceiling fan? Keep going, listening for the faintest of sounds, as long as you can.

Use Your Sense of Touch to Bring In the Moment

Use your sense of touch in a deliberate, self-disciplined way. Close your eyes. Is there any movement of air in the room? Can you feel it against your face, neck, or hands? It may require deep concentration to tune in to this sensation. What else do you feel? How do your clothes feel in contact with your skin? Can you feel their weight on your shoulders or their texture against your legs? Can you feel the weight of a watch or bracelet on your wrist, the weight of the shoes on your feet? Think about everything in contact with your skin, beginning with your feet. Do you feel a breeze against bare skin? Pressure of warm socks? Are they too tight? Or do you feel only the pressure of sheets across your bare feet?

Next, think about the skin on your legs, then your torso and arms, as you slowly move up your body. Pay close attention to your hands. They are very sensitive and can pick up the slightest movements of air. Reach out with your hands and feel the texture of things around you. What does the chair you're sitting on feel like? The sheets on your bed? The pulp of the paper of this page? Your face is also sensitive to air currents and temperature. What do you feel? The weight of your hair across your scalp? Tingling? As you take in these sensations, you have entered the moment. You are momentarily delivered from your painful thoughts.

Use Your Sense of Taste and Smell

You can practice this exercise at meals, experiencing the sensations of every bite. Between meals, you can try to discern the more subtle smells and tastes. Concentrate on what the inside of your mouth tastes like. Is it a neutral taste? Minty? Smoky? As you inhale, do you notice any changes? Upon inhaling, can you detect the scent of wood? Of dirt? Of cleaning agents? Of fruit? Use your senses of taste and smell to bring you out of your thoughts and into the moment. Jon Kabat-Zinn suggests taking a single raisin into your mouth and chewing and tasting it for ten minutes or so, experiencing every possible taste and physical sensation.

Focus on Your Breathing

Feel your chest rise and fall, the air filling your lungs, your diaphragm expanding, then release it all. Can you feel the air as it exits your nostrils? Concentrate on the muscles that work to draw your every breath, on the air moving in and out of your lungs. If abandonment's panicky feelings draw you away, try exerting greater focus by counting your breaths, perhaps thirty at a time. Most people are able to hold the moment very briefly when they are in the amygdala-driven throes of shattering. The natural tendency is to slip back into obsessive thoughts. Refocus by using one of your senses whenever you notice that your panic has plucked you out of the moment. Staying in the moment is a skill requiring deliberate effort. Try to extend these brief interludes as long as you can and start again each time you recognize that the moment has slipped away. As you develop this skill, using the moment as your mantra, it becomes habit of mind—a habit that helps to short-circuit an emotional hijack.

Engage in Activities in the Moment

Be devoted to creating activities that are experienced in the moment. Try seeking out the most beautiful place you can find and drink it in with your ears, your eyes, your skin, your breath, and your nose, using one sense at a time. Listen to your favorite music, deliberately tracking one of its voices to stay intently focused. Listen to tapes for guided meditation. Keep good reading material on hand, books that will hold your interest and inspire you From time to time, lift your mind from the tape or book to take in the moment's sensations around you. Journal writing is something you accomplish in the moment and an excellent way to zero in, find your center, and focus on your path. It's also a chance to create an action plan for the day and even plan your new life.

The more you practice staying in the moment, the better you become at serenely facing the reality at hand and moving forward. The moment is a state of being that Zen Buddhists and other spiritual orders have aspired to for centuries. To learn to live your life with this kind of mindfulness is to accept change and participate in the joy, love, and bounty of life around and within you. Each time you use the moment as nature's greatest refuge from pain, you strengthen your ability to accept life on life's terms. Science is revealing other ways to create beneficial changes. For each stage of the abandonment program, there are exercises that build on this one, each layer amplifying the benefits along the way.

The severing has cut through the dense tissues of attachment, right through to the molten core of self. Like it or not, you are in touch with your deepest needs and feelings. This is where a whole new life can start. The pain of shattering is an epiphany. Abandonment cuts so deep it feels like a mortal wound, but as you have seen, it arouses your instinct for survival. Cut off and alone, you cry out. You feel primal need and fear. These are the most valuable and important feelings you have. They represent your most elemental needs that have been with you since birth. As you learn to manage the pain, it is important to listen to your fears. They tell you what you need. When you dare to accept these feelings, you are ready to begin to heal.

Akeru allows you to transform the piercing pain of abandonment into an opening. At no other time are you more open and conscious of your center than when abandonment makes it sting. This allows you to bring the very center of yourself into the moment where deep healing resides. You become more present and accessible to others, to life, and to the child within. This child is free to experience sensations, its eyes and ears and skin not yet so well defended against life experience. For the adult as well as the child, all the sensations of life are most intensely felt in the moment. It is this reawakened self that you bring into the moment with you—along with the openness, wonder, and discovery of the child.As you emerge from the shattering state, you have taken significant steps in the direction of emotional self-reliance. You have learned: step one, to understand the depth and nature of your abandonment wound; step two, to acknowledge its pain; step three, to avoid shame by accepting your feelings as natural; step four, to affirm your strength—you can stand alone; and step five, to manage your feelings by getting into the moment.

Shattering is a rite of passage similar to the initiation rights of the shaman who journeys to the spiritual world and wrestles with demons before he can own his power. Some of best healers in our society are those who have been through overwhelming trauma, because they have worked through their shattering.

STAGE TWO: WITHDRAWAL

The withdrawal stage is like being in withdrawal from an addiction. It is when you crave the other person after the initial shock of separation has worn off. Mediated by the brain's own opioid system, what you feel is similar to what addicts feel when they can't get a fix. During the worst of it, you can't get away from your conviction that without your lost loved one, your life is over. This belief comes from the child within you. The child keeps telling you that you must get your loved one to come back at all costs, or you'll die. A primary relationship is a matter of survival for a child; no infant can exist without its nurturer. Urged by the child, you may try to reconnect with your lost partner many times. Even if you don't take action, you fantasize about it. You keep going back because you're still not convinced that the one who's left is no good for you. You keep getting bruised, but the child inside believes that this time will be different. You're like the alcoholic who thinks next time he drinks, he won't get drunk. You may get angry with others who try to nurture you. You may, for instance, lash out at your therapist, especially if she is encouraging you to stay away from your old partner. You may have agreed to leave the relationship behind, but the child may act out by missing sessions, switching sponsors, or changing recovery groups. You're angry at your therapist and others because they speak against the wishes of the child. The child fears that unless its urgent pleas are heard, its life is in peril.

The child within clings to false hope because it's helpless against feelings of isolation, banishment, and loss. Without hope, you stay buried in despair, and these feelings evolve into profound grief, creating a bottomless well of tears. But with the tears something else is released. Making its way to your consciousness, through memories of the times you were left unprotected and rejected, is your right to be loved. Withdrawal is the stage when you listen to the child's cries. You recognize that her needs are your needs; that you must nurture your most important feelings.

There are those who try to bypass the withdrawal stage with a replacement for their lost love. But withdrawal is not the time for replacement—that will come soon enough—it is the time to accept yourself and your needs.

Keaton's Withdrawal

It had been six weeks since Gabby packed up and left Keaton—suddenly and without warning. Six weeks since that evening he found a lengthy good-bye note on the just-emptied dresser. He woke up in the dark, as he had each morning since she left, wishing he could go back to sleep but knowing that the adrenaline coursing through his body would not let him. It was three A.M. Instantly, he was flooded with panic. He had been through this before, more times than he wished to remember. He just couldn't seem to get a relationship to last. It always ended the same way—eventually she broke up with him. But he didn't expect it with Gabby. He had felt so sure of her.

Here he was again, writhing in his bed, drenched in anxiety, tormented by loneliness, discarded by somebody he'd loved. How would he ever get through this? As he tossed and turned, Gabby inhabited every corner of Keaton's mind. The craving, longing, and yearning for her were unbearable. Finally, early-morning light began to creep into his room. Getting ready for work helped to push her out of his mind for a brief moment. Today, he thought, he would get to work on time. He would go through the motions as best he could, focus, function, and act as normal as possible. Everyone at work knew Gabby had left him. They knew why he'd lost weight and looked so down. He knew what they thought: "It's been six weeks, Keaton. Get it together, already. Snap out of it!"

Keaton was in withdrawal. The more time that passes, the longer your needs go unmet, the more your body and mind ache for all that you've lost. No matter how hard people try to hold themselves together, a profound sense of loss intrudes on every waking moment. The effects of withdrawal are cumulative and wavelike. They often have to get worse before they can get better, a point lost on friends who expect to see your desperation dissipate, not mount day after day.

Keaton tried to tough it out as best he could, but he succumbed to frequent bouts of crying and found it unbearable to be alone. Friends and family tried to keep him company and offer support in the beginning, but they grew frustrated when they saw that he wasn't moving forward or able to pick himself up by his own bootstraps after a few weeks. At least that's how he imagined they saw it. They said things like, "Just let go and move forward," which left him feeling judged and more alone. The fact is, love withdrawal doesn't operate on a schedule; it varies from person to person, situation to situation.

Keaton's abandonment legacy began in early childhood. His father was highly critical, berating him for every mistake and shortcoming. No matter how hard Keaton tried, it was never enough to please his father. He learned to feel disappointed in himself for not doing better in school, sports, or anything else. Whenever his father blew up at him, he blamed himself for not being good enough. As a teenager, Keaton didn't shake the feeling that he needed to prove himself. He was extremely sensitive to rejection.

When his first girlfriend broke up with him at seventeen, he became severely depressed. The romantic rejection brought up all of the old feelings of inadequacy, confirming his deeply held belief that he was unworthy of anyone's love. Overwhelmed with confusion and pain, he drowned his feelings in alcohol. What followed was a chain of relationships gone bad from which he emerged an alcoholic.

At the time Gabby had left him, Keaton had been in Alcoholics Anonymous for more than five years. In spite of being sober, he still suffered the scourge of romantic rejection. "I had already been through too many abandonments," said Keaton. "It felt like I was in advanced relationship failure—like I had a progressive disease—called rejection. My future seemed hopeless. I couldn't stop beating myself up for all the mistakes I made in my relationship with Gabby, damning myself for being such a failure with her, with everybody else, and with my life."

Withdrawal is the second stage of abandonment. The word describes the pain and longing you feel now that you have separated from the one you loved. Withdrawal can set in immediately, or you may not feel its pull until the numbness and shock of shattering have worn off. As you saw with Keaton, withdrawal overlaps into the next stage, internalizing, in which you take your frustrations out on yourself. As you swirl through the abandonment cycle, you may revisit the symptoms of withdrawal many times. I am going to share some of my own experiences with the withdrawal stage and take you on a journey through the feelings and situations you'll encounter, providing information along the way that will help you understand the process and how to cope with it. I will explain how love withdrawal is a legitimate form of addiction withdrawal and discuss some of the post-traumatic aspects of withdrawal. Hopefully, you'll be able to identify unfinished business left over from your earlier experiences with love withdrawal. Finally, I'll show you how to maximize the growth potential of the withdrawal stage, introducing you to the second Akeru exercise designed to help you to recover and benefit from withdrawal feelings, both old and new.

Withdrawal is life without the medication of your lost relationship. You are coming down from the sedation of security to face reality. Symptoms of withdrawal are intense. Many abandonment survivors are prepared to bargain, petition, beg, manipulate, do anything to get their loved one to come back. During this stage you are like the addict desperate for the love fix you can't get. You're strung out. Instead of a drug, you're jonesing for the person. What are these intense feelings of yearning, agonizing, and craving about? Relationships are, in fact, mediated by the brain's own opioid system. Most people are familiar with the opiate drugs, narcotics like morphine, heroin, and opium. Our brains produce their own morphinelike substances, including endorphin. Both narcotics and the brain's own natural opioids help to block pain.

According to researcher Jaak Panksepp, when you build a close relationship, your brain produces certain opioids that mediate attachment. Although produced naturally in the body, these opioids are as highly addictive as heroin. Their role is nothing short of pair bonding and adhering you to others in the service of species survival. When a relationship ends, the production of certain opioids decreases, and your body goes through physical withdrawal. Biochemically speaking, then, your closest relationships are a form of endorphin addiction. What you feel during abandonment withdrawal—the craving, yearning, waiting, and wanting of your lost loved one—is psychobiologically akin to withdrawal from heroin or morphine. The difference is that when you are in love withdrawal, you associate your symptoms with your emotional loss rather than with a narcotic. In other words, the difference is the context—how you interpret the withdrawal symptoms—not the physical symptoms themselves.

What are some of these withdrawal symptoms?

Wrenching Apart

Even if your relationship is completely over and you have already been through the devastating

breakup, you still face the process of wrenching apart. You are wrenching apart from the need for that person, from the presence of that person in your thoughts, hopes, and dreams, and from your future with that person.

"During withdrawal, it felt like I had been amputated from my conjoined twin," said Marie.

"Shattering was the surgery without anesthesia. It was involuntary surgery. He was the one who decided to have me severed from him and I was the one left in the recovery room, bleeding to death, crying out in pain for my other half."

You'll alternate between moments when you think you might survive without your lost love and moments of total despair. Even if the relationship had been only a date or two, your hopes for the future and your need for love were invested in that person. When hopes don't materialize, your disappointment can be profound; it puts you right back where you were before: alone. Your sense of loss may be no less painful than if you had been married for many years.

Human beings are social creatures. We all need to feel we belong. Building a relationship is one way in which we fulfill that need. You may have taken it for granted, but belonging to someone was essential to your sense of well-being. It felt good to know that you were an important part of his or her life—that someone loved and cherished you. Even if you had just begun to date the person, the prospect of life without that relationship is fraught with desperation and loss.

"I thought I had finally found someone," explained John. "But she never returned my text. It turned out to be just a reminder of how alone I was, how empty my life really was, how much I needed to have love in my life. Just one date and it threw my whole life into emotional crisis."

Without

Being in withdrawal is being without—without the security and nurturance that you counted on or hoped for.

"I had no idea how much my wife meant to me until she left," said Richard. "Our relationship had been in the doldrums for a long time. We bickered constantly. There was always tension in the air. But when she said she needed space, and then actually got an attorney, I felt as if the bottom dropped out of my life and I couldn't find any reason to live anymore." The irony is that people can be as devastated by the loss of a bad relationship as they are by the loss of a good one. Exploring why that is so is central to understanding the abandonment experience. Why is the loss of a primary relationship so awful? How did we become so dependent on another person? Why do we feel incomplete now that they're gone from our lives? The answer to that question is never simple. The fact is, mates and lovers fulfill a whole variety of complex needs; they are much more than companions or lovers or sexual partners. One of those most important roles they play is acting as background object.

Background Object

Our mothers or primary caretakers became background objects for us when we were two or three years old and began exploring the world beyond their embrace. We were content to roam freely so long as we knew Mommy's lap was just a call away. As adults, having someone in the background fulfills a similar need. A background object is the person from whom we derive our primary sense of connectedness, belonging, and security.

If your relationship was like most, having your mate in the background meant that even when you weren't physically together, you enjoyed the security of knowing they were there. They were someone to come home to at the end of a long day or to lie down next to at night or just to think about. It is a feeling that is very easy to take for granted—that sense of belonging and security. It's also inextricably entwined with our most basic needs. It's like oxygen. We can't survive without it but we don't focus on taking it in. "Redington traveled between England and Brazil," said Hope. "We spoke on the phone about twice a week—just to call each other special pet names and say our I-love-you. And then each of us went back to our separate lives, perfectly content, knowing we belonged to each other."

Many people function as well as they do precisely because they feel so secure in their primary relationships. They are self-confident, self-directed, and content because they know someone is there for them. They have a safety net, a "go-to" person. The fact that we tend to take our loved ones for granted isn't a character flaw. The element of security they provide is the very thing that enables us to tolerate separation from them as we make strides in our careers and other pursuits. One mark of a mature relationship is when each partner is able to give the other person space. They allow each other to function as background objects. These folks recognize that their significant others are part of their lives, important, but not their whole life.

When the honeymoon is over, many couples often settle into a period of complacency. Perhaps one or both will even gain weight as the adrenaline and urgency to bond abate and the relationship becomes more secure. This state of relaxation involves the parasympathetic branch of the autonomic nervous system (mediated by the left prefrontal cortex), which works to rebalance the body when the sympathetic nervous system has been aroused. The parasympathetic system helps to get your blood pressure and stress hormone levels back to baseline and turns other life-sustaining systems, like your appetite, back on. Ideally, this sustained period of complacency allows the couple to become industrious as they prepare for the future: start a family, build their careers. Each will operate in his or her own sphere yet bring something from that sphere to the relationship, too.

As we become secure enough in a relationship to take our partner's presence for granted, we may even indulge in fantasies about being with someone else. Such fantasies are not always a sign of trouble. They can add an element of excitement to a relationship in the doldrums. They are fantasies, after all. The reality of a lost partner is very different. To better understand why background objects are so important, let's look at how children learn to function independently. As a young child, you needed to connect in order to move forward. As an infant, you depended on your mother to give nurturance, and your attention focused almost exclusively on that relationship. When you were a toddler, she became a background object as you began to function more independently. You progressed from needing your Mommy figure in your sights at every moment to a stage where you could play by yourself for hours, alone or with other children, as long as you could reassure yourself that Mommy was still around—somewhere in the background. If something interfered with that development—if Mommy had to go to the hospital for a long stay—your ability to work independently at school may have been delayed, and you may have needed constant prompting by the teacher to stay on task. Most of us trusted that our mothers were there to support us. That trust is what enabled us to withstand separation from her. Eventually, you built up enough trust to endure the stress of leaving her side to go to school. The key to taking that step was to trust that your caretaker was at home waiting for your return. Children occasionally question that trust and cry out for reassurance. A child with a stomachache may want to go home to be with Mommy. As adults, we're capable of regression, too. On some level we all need to be reassured of connections to our loved ones. Sometimes that takes the form of phone calls or texts; other times you need their arms around you.

You may not have realized just how much you depended on these reassurances until the relationship is over. You may have downplayed how much you needed your partner, preferring to think of yourself as emotionally self-reliant. The fact is, expressing need and vulnerability are as essential to your psychological functioning as independence. Vulnerability awakened by abandonment is not a weakness; it is part of what it is to be human.

"I didn't realize how important Redington's weekly phone calls had been," said Hope, "until he called me the last time from Brazil to say that he had met someone. Then I found my independent life suddenly didn't work for me. I needed him to be right there with me like I never needed him before. But he was gone, and I was totally lost and insecure. My life was suddenly an empty existence." It's easy for us to underestimate our basic human need for connection. We live in relative isolation from one another, often far from extended family. When we lose our primary relationship, we are not cushioned by the support of a close-knit society as our ancestors were. The sense of deprivation is nearly total because so many of our needs were vested in that one person. Try as we might, we cannot will those needy feelings away.

Will To Run Riot

Abandonment is a form of involuntary separation. The fact that you did not choose to be alone arouses intense feelings of anger, frustration, and resentment. Your partner has upset your emotional balance, and as a result of his or her default, you are alone. Remember that you're not railing against aloneness itself; the circumstances surrounding your sudden isolation are what cause your will to run riot. You are unable and unwilling to accept the conditions of your imposed isolation. You have no control over it, at least for the time being. During the withdrawal stage, you are feeling your partner's absence on many levels. You have emotionally lost the person you loved; you are physically apart, and perhaps worst of all, you are left to contemplate your future alone.

Being alone is not a disease or a social problem. It is a lifestyle preferred by many. In fact, more and more people are choosing to remain single, preferring to create composite lives out of career, friends, pets, clubs, and other interests. Over the ages, spiritual orders around the globe attest to the benefits of solitary living and even celibacy. They provide inspiration for those whose life energy is no longer invested in a primary relationship. But for those of you in the withdrawal stage, being alone is unfamiliar and unwelcome; you are not emotionally prepared to appreciate its benefits. You may have chosen to be alone. That's the whole point: It wasn't against your will. But if you didn't choose it, you are indeed faced with a battle of your will. Once you are able to resolve that battle—once you are able to get past your angry protest—you may come to look upon being alone with a more positive attitude. As you resolve the anger about being left, you begin to take advantage of what your temporary aloneness has to offer. This can be a time of healing solitude, a time to restore your emotional reserves, and a time of personal reflection. Perhaps it is time to question the complacency of your former life, to decide what is truly important to you.

The fear that you have been condemned to a solitary existence may be holding you back. You grieve over your lost love so keenly during this stage that it is hard to imagine becoming attached to anyone or anything else in life that will make you feel whole again. The sense that you will always be alone is one of abandonment's most potent feelings. But remember, it is a feeling, not a prophecy or a fact. The truth is, very few people going through abandonment are destined to be alone for very long. As my clients begin to heal, I encourage them to make new connections as soon as possible, to go outside their usual social circles and widen their scope of activities, to reach out to new people and share their growing self-awareness. I'll discuss making connections in greater depth in Chapter 7.

In the meantime, it is important to realize that only when you stop fighting the fact that you're alone can you recognize its purpose in your emotional recovery. First you must work your way through your feelings of outrage, shock, and betrayal. Slowly you tap inner strength to get through the isolation. You truly stand on your own two feet. The concept of Akeru is there to remind you that "to empty, to make a hole in" is also to create a new beginning. Being alone forces you to become more self-reliant. In the end, you count your time alone as an accomplishment that bolsters self-esteem.

"At first I thought I would die of loneliness," said Marie. "But now that I have gotten over the initial shock, I realize that my life is exactly where it needs to be right now to allow me to work on the things about myself that I need to. For whatever reason I'm alone right now, I've decided to flip it—to find the good in it."

Sexual Withdrawal

Another commonly reported symptom of this stage is sexual withdrawal. When your body's self-defense system is activated, a number of body functions are shut down. Your energy is reserved for self-preservation. In crises, one of the areas to shut down is your reproductive system, a system that normally consumes a great deal of your body's energy. Your sexual drive usually decreases: Females are less likely to ovulate; males may have trouble with erections and secrete less testosterone. Yet abandonment survivors commonly report a heightened craving for sex, particularly for sex with their lost love. They may have more sexual fantasies, pursue sexual activity with substitute partners, or masturbate more often as a way of soothing withdrawal symptoms. Many make repeated sexual overtures to their old partners in the hope of seducing them back into the relationship. Your primitive core needs have been triggered, encompassing the sucking reflex and the need to be held.

"After Lonny was gone for a few weeks," said Marie, "pandemonium set in. I went into sexual withdrawal—a whole new torture to deal with. Suddenly I had the urge to make love to Lonny like never before.

"I had sexual dreams that were so powerful and agonizing that they woke me up, and I wouldn't be able to get back to sleep. I went shopping for lingerie just in case I got the chance to seduce him. The desire was unbearable."

The component of sexual fantasy is only one aspect of the larger issue of physical withdrawal. Abandonment survivors are often embarrassed by their heightened sexual cravings and don't mention them to friends or therapists. Also, these extremely personal feelings may not seem relevant in the face of the other overriding issues they are being bombarded with on a day-by-day basis. Generally, heightened sexual needs tend to taper off as you make your way through the withdrawal stage.

WEIGHT LOSS

Many lose weight immediately after a breakup and continue to drop pounds or establish a lower then normal set point. Your general lack of appetite is interspersed with sudden bouts of ravenous hunger, which help make up for the meals you've missed. Soon after, the butterflies and queasy feeling return and you lose interest in food again.

"I wouldn't feel like eating all day," said Roberta. "And then I'd have a craving for spareribs, something I ordinarily wouldn't touch with a ten-foot pole. But I'd devour them like an animal, grabbing meat off the bone with my teeth as grease poured down my fingers and face." There's a biological explanation for why some people go on feeding frenzies while others seem to be on hunger strikes. Your abandonment crisis boosts production of significant stress hormones. According to physiologist Robert Sapolsky, CRF (corticotropin releasing factor) and ACTH (adrenocorticotropic hormone) prepare your fight-or-flight response by shutting down your appetite and other digestive processes. Your salivary glands stop secreting, and your stomach goes to sleep. You notice a dry mouth and queasy stomach. This shutdown helps to divert energy to your major muscles—the ones that enable you to sprint across the savannah to escape a predator, or engage in battle, if need be.

Glucocorticoids, another group of stress hormones, are also involved in your self-defense response. These hormones appear to stimulate appetite rather than suppress it. Sapolsky's tests showed this effect in laboratory rats, but the effect is probably the same for humans. When your amygdala detects a crisis, CRF and ACTH are released first, preparing you to act quickly, if necessary. Next, levels of glucocorticoids begin to build. Glucocorticoids also increase your appetite, encouraging you to rebuild your energy stores in the event that an attacker poses an ongoing threat. Timing helps to explain why some lose their appetites while others can't stop eating.

Wakefulness

Because a breakup is an ongoing emotional emergency, most people continue to have trouble sleeping during the withdrawal stage. They report feeling anxious when they wake and tend to get up earlier than normal. Others stay in bed later (though they don't sleep well) and are drowsy later in the day when they are normally most active.

"I just couldn't face the day," said Roberta. "I'd still be in bed at three in the afternoon on weekends, and only got up because my lower back would start aching from lying around. Anyway, I was probably wiped out, because I was still waking up in the middle of the night, drenched in those cold sweats of panic."

These interruptions in your normal sleep patterns are explained by the same processes that affect your appetite. Your body continues to secrete stress hormones that keep you awake and "action ready," even at night. You're alert and prepared as though a predator is still lurking about.

Waiting And Watching

One of the hallmarks of withdrawal is waiting for the lost loved one to return. This expectant feeling is common to all types of grief. Even when a loved one has died and there is no chance he or she will return, the mourner's emotional brain goes through a period of hopeful anticipation of the return of the departed. From a biochemical standpoint, searching and yearning are the emotional expressions of opioid withdrawal.

What accounts for this deeply entrenched pattern? Forming attachments, is a powerful biological mandate. When your loved one is torn away, you feel the loss immediately and deeply. During withdrawal, your mind automatically seeks an emotional bond it can no longer find. This seeking is your emotional brain (your mammalian or limbic brain) trying to recapture what it is conditioned to believe is necessary for your survival. Try as you might to control this, you are usually unable to stop the futile search for the person whom your rational mind knows is no longer there. In spite of your efforts to regain your composure, your mind goes right on searching for your lost partner. It is as if your loss were an amputation of a limb, and you are suffering the effects of intense phantom pain.

The waiting and watching for your lost loved one is the result of your amygdala preparing you for hyper vigilance—to be alert and on the lookout for any signs of your old partner. Your body prepares you for this sustained vigil. Your pupils involuntarily dilate so you can better see the object of your concern. Your hearing and other senses are more acute as well, hence the tendency to jump at the slightest noise. Your conscious mind is preoccupied with all matters pertaining to the missing person, assisting your emotional brain in its search. You look through photos and gifts that remind you of your time together, perhaps retracing the last moments of contact, hoping to discover clues to why it had to end. You may even feel compelled to go to the actual places where you met. These visits evoke memories that provide fresh clues for your brain's relentless search.

"At the beginning," said Marie, "I just had a need to drive past Lonny's apartment at night, to see if his car was there. Somehow, I felt less anxious if I could at least keep track of his whereabouts. If his light was on, he was found. I knew where he was. If not, he was lost, and I'd become frantic. Where could he be? He was out there lost somewhere." Your tendency to mistake others for your lost partner can reach an all-time high. You imagine that you see your lost loved one at a distance, in a crowd. As you approach, of course, it turns out to have been an illusion.

Accepting loss is a slow and painful process, and you spend a great deal of time and emotional energy before your intense searching effort gives way to reality, and your mind's waiting game is finally over. You must accept the reality of your loss not just rationally (usually easy enough) but on psychobiological levels—including those beneath your conscious awareness—before this vigilant state begins to subside. The second Akeru exercise will help you do this.

Washed Out, Miserable, And Depressed

Withdrawal symptoms represent stage two of your separation trauma, a continuation of your psychobiological distress that began with shattering. Withdrawal takes its toll over time, wearing you down, depleting your energy supplies.

"I had trouble dragging myself to work," said Roberta. "I had this horrible vulnerable feeling all of the time like something bad was set to happen any minute. I was stressed out and ready to drop. I even thought I might have mono or chronic fatigue syndrome or some other mysterious ailment. But my blood tests came back negative."

The continued loss of appetite, intermittent wakefulness, hypervigilance, relentlessness, and searching for your lost partner are all signs of post-traumatic stress. Many also report having intense dreams that leave them flooded with anxiety or profound desolation upon awakening. Experiencing one or all of these symptoms doesn't mean you are going to develop a full-blown case of post-traumatic stress disorder. Your body is endowed with self-corrective mechanisms (mediated by the left frontal cortex), and many of these symptoms will subside. In the meantime, the experience can be overwhelming.

Withdrawal Stage Is Post-Trauma

Abandonment isn't like an automobile accident from which you immediately begin to recover. It is more like spending weeks or months on a battlefield, constantly under attack. You feel the painful repercussions of your loss again and again each time your ever-wary amygdala triggers the release of stress hormones. Abandonment poses an additional complication: reopening of old wounds. For those who lived through some kind of childhood separation, going through the withdrawal stage means dealing with the emotional reverberations of the recent and past wounds simultaneously. They merge together into one prolonged state of emotional emergency, a tumultuous and intense time of great stress. As Richard put it, "We are surrounded with the blood, gore, death, and dismemberment of our whole lives."

Upon hearing this, Keaton joked, "Don't you think, Richard, that that's a bit understated?" Your lost relationship helped to regulate many psychobiological functions. It is almost impossible to say how many aspects of your emotional and hormonal health were dependent on it, since so much of it happened beneath your conscious awareness. But in fact, you had become entwined with that person in complex ways.

The relationship met countless needs that helped to maintain your state of equilibrium. You incorporated your loved one into your thoughts and plans and made countless adjustments in your behavior in order to achieve as balanced a relationship as possible. As your attachment formed over time, you achieved what researchers call a state of attunement. Being attuned means that you and your partner's pupils dilated in synchrony, you echoed each other's speech patterns, movements, and even cardiac and EEG rhythms. As a couple, you functioned like a mutual biofeedback system, stimulating and modulating each other's biorhythms. You had even grown accustomed to each other's pheromones, chemicals that human beings (as well as other animals) emit into the air. A small organ within the human nose (the vomeronasal organ) detects their presence. This organ is distinct from the olfactory organ for smell. The detection of one another's pheromones represents a sixth sense that has been found to regulate menstrual cycles and play a role in human attraction. Needless to say, your relationship maintained your social, emotional, and physical well-being on all different levels.

Now that the relationship is over, the many processes that it helped regulate are in disarray. It is during withdrawal that the effects begin to express themselves cumulatively, creating a mounting feeling of agitation. It is difficult to isolate how a single body system is affected, since the body's systems interact to form a complex web. I've tried to do so with the brain's opioid system (separation distress has been found to lead to a reduction in certain opioids, and to symptoms of withdrawal akin to heroin withdrawal) and with the stress hormones (which affect appetite, sleep, and other states of alertness and action readiness). But in fact, stress hormones influence many other functions as well, including the immune system, the growth process, aging, memory, energy levels, and moods. Sustained arousal of the body's fight-or-flight response is associated with anxiety. Increased levels of glucocorticoid and CRF stress hormones are found in people diagnosed with depression.

Hormonal, neurotransmitter, opioid, and other biochemical levels usually return to baseline as you progress through the stages of recovery. In the meantime, you are left to contend with your body's sustained state of arousal, along with the practical challenges you face. It is no small wonder that you are temporarily washed out, stressed out, miserable, and depressed. During withdrawal, you are fighting an enormous aggressive mental battle, exerting as much energy as if you were actually wrestling with a powerful enemy.

Step one: Your first task is to create a vivid picture of your abandoned child, that newly awakened part of yourself. Recall yourself as a very young child (of about four) and use that image to personify your emotional core. Imagine that you, the adult, can stand back and observe this child, as if he or she is a separate being, standing outside you. This helps to cognitively draw the needy feelings this child represents out from where they are hidden within your limbic brain. Robertiello and Kirsten recommend that you picture this child standing five feet away from you on your weaker side. If you are right-handed, that means on your left side. The idea is to remind you that your child self is in fact more vulnerable and dependent than your adult self.

The child has long been within you, making its needs known in the form of intrusive anxiety that can interfere in your relationships and life. By creating a separate identity for this child, you create a safe container for your most deeply buried feelings, where you can bring them to greater consciousness, and finally tend to them effectively. The idea is to attribute all of your feelings—those you are aware of and those you hope to discover— to your child self. When you feel insecure it is the child within you who is insecure, the child who feels desperate for acceptance and approval. It is also the child who is afraid to take risks and the child whose anxiety can float free from its source and dampen your mood or overwhelm you with feelings of neediness. Rather than become angry at these feelings (this would forsake the child), your task is to finally accept and care for this long-abandoned part of yourself. You learn to be comfortable with (and bring comfort to) your uncomfortable feelings—a big step.

It is critical to avoid blaming your self-defeating behaviors on your inner child's feelings, no matter how intrusive and uncomfortable they may be. Feelings are involuntary. Feelings are never the problem; they are given. It is how you handle them that can cause the problem. Self-sabotage is the domain, not of the inner child, but of the outer child—the hidden self-saboteur I will introduce you to in the chapter on rage. The outer child, not the inner child, is the part that acts out your insecurity and rage inappropriately and interferes in your relationships. Attributing this self-defeating behavior to your outer child leaves your inner child free to receive all of your unqualified love and acceptance.

Separation therapy requires that you keep feelings separated from behavior—inner from outer—so that you can hold your inner child blameless for any self-sabotage its feelings may have triggered. The idea is to encourage this child self to express all of its feelings, even powerfully negative ones such as desperation and panic. Accepting and administering to these feelings is how to best show unconditional love toward yourself. The process reverses self-hatred—a virulent form of self-abandonment. You learn to complete your own emotional loop rather than overwhelm others with your emotional needs.

Step two: Now visualize your adult self.

Form a picture in your head of the person you wish to become. "I had a hard time visualizing my adult self," said Keaton. "I wasn't too comfortable with him. In fact, I didn't even like him. He had let me down too many times." Keaton's difficulty is common. Many struggle at first when they try to see themselves as a strong, capable adult, but recent science shows such an effort to be well worth it. Creating the mental image of Big You—personifying your adult self—stimulates recently discovered brain cells that neuroscientists call mirror neurons.

Mirror neurons perform remarkable functions that have only recently come into focus. They are instrumental in developing empathy and learning new skills. When you observe someone doing something, or visualize yourself doing it, the mirror neuron system activates the same areas of the brain that would light up if you were actually taking that action. They allow your brain to create a neurological facsimile— a trial run—thereby increasing your skills in that area as if you were actually practicing in real time. The same is true when you observe someone expressing an emotion, or imagine yourself having that emotion.

It stimulates your mirror neuron system and allows you to experience that emotion. This increases your emotional range and strengthens your capacity for empathy.

Because of the plasticity of the brain, this stimulation can promote significant neural development. The exercise asks you to visualize yourself as a stronger adult in the act of showing caring and compassion toward your inner child. You create mental images of yourself performing effective self nurturing acts on your own behalf. As you practice this exercise, you inculcate self-love, something that has heretofore belonged in the easier-said-than-done bin. The exercise also has practical benefit in that it increases the skill sets, confidence, and preparedness you need to ultimately follow through and reach your goals.

To create a mental image of your higher adult self, you might begin by picturing yourself doing something you know you are reasonably good at and then build from there. Keaton was able to overcome his difficulties by remembering himself playing poker one night when he'd played a winning hand for all it was worth, feeling confident and competent.

Marie recalled herself having made lasagna one evening and confidently serving it to a room full of friends, feeling beloved, centered, and self-possessed. Think of the times you knew you were at your best, most competent, and independent. From these positive recollections as well as your future aspirations, form a composite image that includes all the best of you and the you that you are becoming. Imagine this higher adult self taking exquisite care of your own needs. Add to this image as you grow.

Step three: Now you're ready to start a dialogue between the adult image of yourself and the child— between Big You and Little You. By creating an image of your child self and potential adult self, you have created a triangle. You, the individual writing the dialogue, are at the top of the triangle. The child is on the bottom left; the adult on the bottom right. You are going to remain at the top as an objective observer, where you can mediate the dialogue between these two figures, between your most urgent needs and the capable adult you know you can become.

The role for the adult self: Your adult self's job is to validate your inner child's feelings and provide all that he or she needs: a sense of belonging and love, to be admired and listened to, to be relieved of guilt and burden. Your adult self should act like a good parent toward a cherished child. The role of the child self: In turn, the child will express its feelings and look to your adult self for help. As you begin to see your child self as a separate figure, this child reveals his or her most basic needs, fears, hopes, and dreams. Many of these things have been buried for a long time. This exercise is designed to bring them out in the open. The role of the individual: As the mediator of the dialogue, you will be conducting a kind of oneperson role-play. You, of course, give voice to both your child self and adult self. When you are speaking for the child, you take on the language and attitude of a child. When you are speaking for the adult, you take on the body language of a strong and sensible adult whose main goal is to help the child.

Your task is to become more aware of what you are feeling. Attribute these feelings to the child. You are also supporting the adult who is striving to be strong and emotionally self-nurturing.

Withdrawal is when all of the connections with our lost love are torn. We try to move forward with loose wires hanging out, exposed and sparking. We were so medicated by the relationship, we didn't realize how intricate our connections had become. Only now can we distinguish which of the wires are part of a healthy connection to our loved one and which were based on fear or the excessive need to please. As we heal, we test the loose wires through soul-searching, therapists, sponsors, friends, and trial encounters with new people. Eventually, we discover the connections to true nurturing and healthy relationships.

Our core feelings are awake and alive—the oldest, most enduring part of ourselves. All else is ripped away. The child on the rock cries out for what is lost. It is this child who feels the wrenching tear in the tissues of attachment, the frustration and intense need to reconnect. When we give the child a voice, we are finally able to administer to the needs, fears, and longings of our innermost self. We reverse self-abandonment. By holding the child blameless for our own acts of self-sabotage and embracing all of his or her feelings, we inculcate unconditional self-love.

During withdrawal we are like the baby chick without its shell, still wet, facing the world without its protective cover. It is the ultimate trial of survival. We are free from the restrictive bonds of security. No longer sedated by our former relationships, we emerge stark and alive, our needs exposed, our feelings raw, to forge new connections. Withdrawal is you becoming you for the first time. It is individuation.

Stage Three: Internalizing the Rejection

Internalizing means incorporating an emotional experience, making it a part of yourself, and letting it change your deepest beliefs. It is an insidious process. You don't realize how much it affects you. Internalizing the rejection is how your body incorporates the wound of abandonment. You have taken it to heart. By internalizing rejection, you injure yourself. During the internalizing stage, the self searches desperately for its lost love, then turns its rage and frustration against itself. The wound becomes a self-contained system where self-doubt incubates and fear becomes ingrown.

Self is the main tool for functioning in the world. To diminish it is to commit self-abandonment. Internalizing is the most critical stage of the abandonment process, when your emotional wound is most susceptible to infection. If you don't tend to the wound, it can damage your self-esteem. It is a time to treat the virulent bacteria of rejection that have left you momentarily weakened. As with shattering and withdrawal, during the internalizing process your old wounds reopen, spilling their toxins in the new sore. But therein lies its benefit. Abandonment is a cumulative wound— rejections past and present merge. It's a time to clean out the insecurities, feelings of worthlessness, and shame that have been festering since childhood. Your task is to dredge up the bottom of the swamp and sift through the muck to salvage what's important. You begin to reconstruct.

Barbara's Internalizing

Barbara was a homemaker and mother of five children all under age ten when her husband left her for another woman, someone he'd met through his business.

"When I asked Howard to tell me about her," says Barbara, "he told me she was a colleague, as if that was supposed to explain everything. 'What does that make me?' I asked him. But I already knew who I was. A dependent housewife with no identity outside him or our family, that's who. We had been married for thirteen and a half years. It never occurred to me that Howard would want to leave. I just didn't have enough worldly sophistication to hold his interest. After all, I had been home with the kids all this time, while he was out making his mark. I must have been the picture of the homely housewife, knee-deep in laundry, soccer practices, and screaming kids.

"I guess I was counting on those perfect pie crusts and that homemade jam to hold Howard's interest. I thought I was being the ideal wife by ironing his shirts and keeping his socks sorted. But I realize I made a big mistake allowing myself to become his servant. That must have been all I meant to him as a bed partner, too. All that lovemaking. It always meant a lot to me, but to him it must have been about as meaningful as physical exercise. I had just been a receptacle. "I know I sound bitter. That is something Howard used to catch me on—negativity. He didn't have that problem—he could let go of things easily. In fact, he never complained about the way I ran the house, though I know I probably could have done a better job. I don't think I yell at the kids more than any other mother, but Howard had no way of knowing that. He probably couldn't stand it, but he kept his mouth shut like the perfect gentleman he always was. If only I'd realized he would someday grow tired of the whole scene and of me, I would have done things differently.

"I was naive enough to believe that all he needed from me was to keep the home fires burning. But he was out in the world, constantly coming into contact with more interesting women. I should have known. He got tired of me, the one he domesticated. He obviously wanted a more equal partner. Actually, I thought I was his equal, but I can't compete with the type of career woman Howard is with now.

"When he calls, he first asks about the children, and then if I found a job. I know I need to work for all of us to be able to survive financially. But I am petrified that I won't be able to do anything. I'm sure my college degree is obsolete by now after all of these years. Who is going to hire me? You need work experience to get a decent job.

"I'm scared, and I know Howard must be right—I'm the one who dug myself into this corner, wanting all of those kids, hiding behind the needs of the family."

Barbara's own account includes many of the "I" words associated with the internalizing process: the self-indictment, the painful introspection, the insecurity about her role, the tendency to idealize the one who has left, her feelings of inadequacy and sexual invisibility, impotence over the circumstances of her life, and the inventory of choices she now regrets. Not all of us make self-deprecating comments out loud the way Barbara does, but many abandonment survivors report feelings similar to hers. In a way, Barbara is fortunate to be conscious of them. As she begins to work through her recovery, this awareness will help her to identify and challenge these negative thoughts. For most, the process of internalizing happens on a deeply personal level, in the privacy of your innermost thoughts. Self-doubt takes its toll silently and over an extended period of time. It becomes the invisible drain that leeches self-esteem from within. Your friends and family probably don't realize that you are going through the potentially most damaging part of the grieving process. Internalizing the rejection is the third phase of abandonment, but its process is at work throughout the grief cycle. Internalizing occurs every time you become angry or frustrated with yourself for letting your partner leave you. And it is painful. Anger turned against yourself accounts for the intense depression associated with abandonment. It is one of the hallmarks of this part of the grief cycle. I'd met Barbara about two months after my own abandonment experience. As I observed her progress, I found myself struggling in the same quicksand of worthless feelings and self-doubt. This internalizing muck can claim anyone's self-esteem, at least temporarily. I was determined that it was not going to get mine.

I tried to make my way through the quagmires of self-deprecation by rationalizing. I had nothing to feel ashamed of, I told myself. I was gainfully employed. My career was intact. I had successfully raised a family. In fact, my youngest child left for college the same month that my partner left me, and I managed to survive the sudden isolation. I tried to reassure myself that I was okay, but it was hard to be convincing. I found myself rambling around in an empty house that a month ago had been bustling with the activity of a loving family.

I knew I had done nothing wrong. I had loved and cared for this man in every way possible. I had upheld my end of things; I'd even maintained an ideal trim weight after all of those years. I'd paid special attention to my clothing, makeup, hair. In fact, I reassured myself looking in the mirror, I looked better now than I did before. Besides, I was wiser, more successful, more seasoned. So, why suddenly weren't my accomplishments enough? Didn't they mean anything? But I was only too familiar with the toxic fumes that rise out of the abandonment wound. Those colorless and odorless gases can seep silently into your consciousness, even when you think you're keeping a positive outlook. As a therapist, I knew I had to break free from the miasma of self-doubt. I began discovering new techniques that are included in this program that helped me resuscitate myself. I tried new activities and broke out of old familiar routines. I began traveling and visiting friends I hadn't seen in a long time. Ultimately I found my roots, recentered myself, and restored my picture of myself. Amazed by the effort it took, I came to truly appreciate the power of the internalizing process. I learned for myself that affirmations were not enough to ward off the impact of the abandonment and its potential damage.

One of the primary tasks of abandonment recovery is to prevent feelings of self-doubt from adhering to your sense of self. I discovered it cannot be done with rational thoughts alone. Bolstering self-esteem requires a more dynamic approach. You need to go with rather than against the internal focus of this stage. If internalizing forces you to become introspective, then take advantage of its centripetal force to bring light and vision along with you. Your goal is to bring positive feelings inward. I am going to take you on a journey through the internalizing process and guide you through the feelings and situations you're likely to encounter along the way. I will explain the significant ways abandonment grief differs from other types of grief, as well as some of the biochemical and hormonal changes that are taking place at this stage. I will also help you identify unfinished business left over from previous losses and outline some of the childhood scenarios that may have affected your self-esteem. Throughout, I will reinforce your central task: to use this time of inward focus to incorporate positive feelings and experiences into your sense of self. Finally, I am going to introduce you to the third Akeru exercise, which tackles injuries to self-esteem that have been holding you back. The goal is to emerge from this introspective time with a stronger sense of self, more capable of life and love than before.

ANATOMY OF ABANDONMENT GRIEF

Up till now, many of the emotions we've discussed—the devastation, shock, and feelings of withdrawal—are feelings we share with those mourning the death of a loved one. During this critical third phase, the special circumstances of abandonment become most apparent, setting it apart from other types of grief. When we think of grieving, we think of a profoundly emotional experience universal to the human condition. The grieving process has been extensively studied and its stages clearly described and defined. It cuts across cultures, genders, ages, and social strata. We even see evidence of these grief stages in other members of the animal kingdom.

As a society we acknowledge grief over a death. But still largely unrecognized is grief over being left. When a friend's mother or husband dies, we expect an extended period of bereavement. We offer social and spiritual support to the mourner. There are no social rituals to comfort abandonment survivors. Your grief may be just as intense and enduring and as financially and emotionally debilitating. Imagine the woman with one bottle of milk left in the refrigerator, three hungry children, no means of supporting them, and a husband who has just flown the coop for another woman. Her concerns go beyond the practical; she is experiencing a complicated grief mixed with rage, a sense of betrayal, and the stigma of being left.

In truth, abandonment grief has not been fully recognized as a legitimate form of grief. Unlike grief over death, which receives serious attention from professionals, abandonment has been psychology's neglected stepchild. Yet like any grief involving loss of a loved one, abandonment is a process that follows its own path. Because it so often goes unrecognized, sufferers often hide it, storing their feelings deep within, where these feelings silently eat away at them, unbeknownst to friends and family, and sometimes even themselves. Many report how isolated they feel, how difficult it is to make others understand what they're going through. Yet this grief can give birth to fear and sadness and diminish self-esteem and life energy for a long time. Unresolved abandonment grief can interfere with future relationships.

A member of a New York Open Center workshop offers this testimonial: "I find it hard to imagine that something that happened ten years ago could still be bothering me," said John. "But after my fiancée broke off our engagement, I didn't know what to do with all of the pain. I guess it stayed with me.

"At the time, it was hard being alone, dangerous even [he had suicidal thoughts], but I hated depending on my friends back then. I got tired playing the victim, so I learned to keep what I was going through to myself. I did what all the self-help books said to do: I tried to let go and move forward, and find happiness from within. I got so good at acting as if everything were okay that I thought I was past it. Just to make sure I would be okay, I avoided relationships so I wouldn't have to be reminded of the feelings. I had no idea that I was grieving. What could I do but try to ignore it?

That's why it's come to haunt me now after ten years—because I'm finally trying to find someone to be with." By hiding his grief, John had become one of abandonment's many walking wounded. He had no obvious injury, but his unrecognized grief silently burdened him for a decade. He had become abandophobic. To better understand what you're going through, it is important to recognize the special features of abandonment grief.

WHAT MAKES ABANDONMENT GRIEF DIFFERENT?

Personal Injury

The crux of the difference between bereavement and abandonment grief has to do with the fact that someone you love has not died but instead has chosen to end your relationship. Your loss is experienced as an affront to your personal worth, rather than an act of nature. When we are rejected by someone important to us, our whole sense of value as a person is thrown into question. Being discarded and disrespected creates a narcissistic injury. A narcissistic injury is a slap in the face, an affront to our pride, to our most personal sense of self, a stinging wound that can leave a deep imprint. Sometimes even apparently insignificant losses such as being overlooked for a promotion or feeling rejected by a friend raise questions about our self-worth. When abandonment involves losing the most important person in our lives, the impact can be devastating.

"After Lonny left," said Marie, "not only did I miss him and miss our lives together, but I missed feeling good about me. I suddenly regretted being me. I felt my confidence go right down the drain." Marie is describing that invisible self-esteem drain that is the hallmark of this phase. Silently, insidiously, self-doubt leeches your sense of worth from within. Unconsciously you begin to interpret new experiences as evidence of your personal inadequacy. The injury to your sense of self is what sets abandonment grief apart from all others.

Grief's Pain

One of the most common misconceptions that abandonment survivors face in the throes of their grief is that their feelings are unjustified, that grieving a death is somehow worse. Abandonment and death affect us in different ways, but it's impossible to say that one is more painful than the other. The intensity and longevity of your grief is related to the nature of your relationship, the circumstances of the loss, and your emotional and constitutional makeup.

"I went to the funeral for the husband of a friend," said Barbara. "I realized as I watched everyone gather around her that I was in as much grief as she was. But there was no dignity about my grief. I had to keep it hidden, all the while participating in a public outpouring of support for her. "It seems that only death qualifies a person to feel this much pain."

Loss

What both types of grief do have in common is loss. The stages of abandonment grief do, in fact, overlap with Kübler-Ross's and Bowlby's stages of grief. Regardless of whether your loss is caused by abandonment or death, losing a loved one disrupts your entire life. You may feel the loss in the middle of the night when you wake up alone, or when your car breaks down and there's no one to pick you up from the repair shop. Losing your partner is like losing a part of yourself. It is like a psychic amputation; you feel intense phantom pain for what is lost. Both abandonment survivors and bereaved spouses alike must grapple with the emotional and practical burdens of facing life alone.

Lack of Social Role and Recognitions

Society, unfortunately, does not assign bereavement roles when someone is abandoned. There is no funeral, there are no letters of sympathy. Rather, you are seen as someone who has been dumped. Abandonment survivors are left to wonder if perhaps they caused their own problems. Maybe it was their fault the relationship ended, perhaps they shouldn't feel such pain, perhaps it's a sign of emotional weakness. These self-recriminations add another layer of shame, forcing us further into emotional exile. "When Lonny left, I felt completely isolated. He wasn't lost to friends or family," says Marie, "he was lost only to me. I was alone in my grief. If he had died instead, then everyone would have lost him. Family and friends would be grieving all over the place. My phone would have been ringing off the hook. People would have been staked out at my house. Everyone would be gathering to give each other support and to support me. After all, I would be the bereaved, the honored one who gets to shut the coffin in the end. And then there would have been a funeral, a grave site, a ritual to mark how sad and tragic it all was.

"Not to mention that the house would be full of sympathy cards and flowers from even our most distant acquaintances. But since Lonny didn't die, it was inappropriate for anyone other than my closest friends and family to acknowledge what I was going through. The rest of the world turned its back, kept a discreet distance. Maybe people didn't want to embarrass me, or maybe they were oblivious to what I was going through. It certainly was not a public matter—because there was no death."

Numbing and Shock

There are issues confronting the bereaved that are different from the ones confronting abandonment survivors. When a loved one dies, we are forced to face our own mortality. Death is absolute, irreversible, and final; the yearning to be reunited with our loved one is fraught with a sense of complete hopelessness and despair. We are so afraid of death, and the idea that we'll never see our partner again is so incomprehensible and terrible that we initially go into shock. As discussed, the brain produces opioids (natural painkillers), which may account for the numbing that grievers report. This numbing helps the bereaved survive the initial trauma, and for some can even create interludes of respite from intense pain. Those who have been left by a loved one also report shock and numbing, but there are differences. Abandonment survivors are not confronted with mortality but rather with the anger and devastation of being left. While they are often numb to life going on around them, they rarely report being numb to the pain of rejection. Instead, they feel unremitting pain. This feeling apparently overrides the pain-numbing effect of the body's opioids.

Anger

Anger is common to both types of grief. Indeed, many experience the death of a loved one as a form of abandonment and openly express their anger over being left behind. Those who have been abandoned are also angry, but for many, the grievance is real. Your loved one voluntarily pulled away. To compound matters, your lost partner may be oblivious to the pain you feel. Often while you are still suffering through the worst of it, your lost partner has already moved on to a new life and perhaps a new lover. So even though your relationship is lost to both of you, the one who was left carries a far greater burden of emotional pain than the one who did the leaving.

As Marie put it, "When Lonny left, I lost the one thing I treasured the most—him. He had all the gold, and I was left with nothing but loss." The bereaved can experience complicated grief when abandonment feelings are present. "My partner had fallen for someone else before she got cancer," wrote Kim in reaching out to my website. "But when she was dying, she welcomed me back with open arms and I loved and cared for her right till the end. Now that she's gone, I'm left feeling somehow unresolved, devalued . . . abandoned. The sting of rejection hurts as much as physically losing her."

Denial

When a loved one dies, the loss is absolutely final. Denial actually helps to ease the person into acceptance. But with abandonment, denial is more complicated. Since your loved one is still alive, you can make contact. In some cases, there might be the possibility for reconciliation. Abandonment survivors' denial, then, can be fueled by realistic possibility. This creates a more active and tenacious kind of searching for the lost object. Where there is breath there is hope, a fact that interferes with closure. This difference does not make abandonment more or less painful than other types of grief, but it means that abandonment survivors may remain in denial and postpone closure, sometimes indefinitely.

Closure

You can attempt what the widow or widower cannot—to get your lost partner to return. The bereaved can only hope to rejoin their loved one on a spiritual plane.

Accepting that their loved one is physically gone is a terrible challenge. Many grievers seek out spiritual mediums in an attempt to visit the other side, where they hope to make contact. For abandonment survivors, the process of closure—of letting go of a relationship—when your lost partner is still alive is that much more difficult.

Love Loss

In grieving over a death, the mourner gets to keep the love of the person who has died, cherishing it, perhaps even feeling comforted by it. In contrast, when a loved one chooses to end a relationship, the love we once felt has been love taken away—perhaps to be given to someone else. It is an ambiguous loss. Love loss and rejection are special kinds of pain that affect your core beliefs about yourself.

Residual Damages

Whether you lose someone because of death or abandonment, the severing is painful and takes time to heal. A workshop member from Manhattan, suffering both types of loss, described the differences: "Death severs you from your loved one with a scalpel. It's a clean cut; it leaves a scar, it's maybe even an amputation. But abandonment is more like shrapnel exploding inside, affecting all of your internal organs. It creates damages that ooze and fester and take forever to heal." One of the goals of abandonment recovery is to recognize abandonment as a legitimate type of grief. It is a grief that has two faces. One is common to all grief; everyone feels loss. The other—the narcissistic injury—sets it apart. There has of course been a great deal written about dealing with loss, and you can draw much value from the work of philosophers and healers.

Building a Self Begin by closing your eyes and imagining that you have unlimited finances at your disposal. Maybe you've won the lottery jackpot. Remember, it's important to stay within the laws of reality. For instance, you can't bring people back from the dead or control other people's behavior (i.e., make them love you), but you can accomplish plenty with enough money. Imagine the ideal setting for the ultimate dreamscape, one so satisfying in its details that you could happily live in it alone if you had to (not that you would have to). What environment would suit these purposes? Does it snow there in the winter months? Or is it tropical? Is it a mountaintop? Does it overlook an ocean, river, lake, or valley? Is it in a dense forest, rural farming area, the city? Is it a cozy neighborhood? An apartment with glorious views? A planned community with built-in amenities? Is it where you live now or in another country?

(Pause, taking time to visualize)

Now start thinking about the structure itself. Remember that money is no object. If small and cozy suits you, so be it. If a mansion is what you have in mind, go for it. The idea is to create a place so ideally suited to your needs that within it you are able to celebrate your separateness as a human being. You and Little will be content to spend your time alone, at peace and happy in this dreamscape. It has everything to satisfy your adult self as well as your child self. If moats or iron fences are what it takes to make you and Little feel secure, include them in your plans. Landscape the property to suit your emotional needs and whims. You may choose to have vast property or perch your house right on the main street of your favorite town.

(Pause)

Now think about the space within the shelter. How much room will you need? No matter what kind of sheltering container you've designed, you will need a place to store or prepare food and a shelter from rain and snow. If it is a house, where is the kitchen? The living space? Is there a library, chapel, observatory, meditation room? What about staircases? Nooks and crannies? Guest quarters? Take a few minutes to think about the quality of the internal space.

(Pause)

Think about your favorite spot within the structure, its heart and soul, the place you spend most of your time, feel most centered and comfortable. Is it the kitchen, sitting at a counter looking at a beautiful view? Leaning against your favorite tree? Or sitting in the den in the most comfortable chair in the world? Once you've decided the emotional center of the dreamscape—your favorite spot—sit yourself down in it, restfully but still fully conscious and alert.

(Pause)

Imagine sitting in your favorite spot and being drawn into the moment by a captivating view. What can you see that makes you feel so totally alive? Taking in this view, you appreciate the importance of existence itself. What is there about it that so enthralls you? A brook? Waterfall? Mountain? Cathedral of trees? Beach? Imagine a view that puts you in touch with life itself and helps you truly live in the moment.

(Pause)

What is the overall feeling of the shelter you are in? Is it filled with light? Does it offer privacy, or is open? What special things are in it? An old potbellied stove? A piano? Seashells? The comforts and pleasures surrounding you should be so complete that this space becomes the one place where you would be able to accept any reality you might be faced with, no matter how difficult, even the one you're dealing with right now. What things draw your attention in a pleasurable way, away from painful thoughts and into the moment? A bird outside the window? The fragrance of flowers? The roar of the ocean? A photograph? A painting?

The space contains these special items, and the view beyond encompasses wondrous elements of nature. Are there horses galloping by? All of it helps you to accept your reality, no matter how challenging.

(Pause)

Create an image of yourself in your dreamscape two years from now feeling peaceful and fulfilled. It is important to imagine yourself engaged in productive future projects to stimulate those mirror neurons. What meaningful activities occupy most of your time? Are you enjoying leisure or an exciting new job? Are you landscaping? Traveling? Painting? Cooking? Arranging family gatherings? Getting a degree? Building a new career? What career? Do you spend a lot of time out of doors?

Visiting friends? Make a special point to conjure up images of yourself engaging in positive activities and feeling good while doing them.

(Pause)

What friends and family would you like to include in your world? Imagine that it's two years from now. Do you have a new significant other, perhaps? Are you with children? Happily living alone? Does anyone—a friend or lover—share the dreamscape with you? In which rooms do you interact with them? Den? Bedroom? Around the kitchen table? Be sure to imagine yourself engaging with people in the way you would like to—making love, snuggling, having fun, or enjoying wonderful conversations. Create a mental image of yourself listening intently to others and caring about them and the warmth you generate.

(Pause)

Imagine that your capacity for love increases every day in this space. All people in your life feel your love. It has warmed a special place within each of them, connecting you with them in deep and meaningful ways. You feel this connection to those next to you and with those far away. This new generosity of spirit flows from your increasing capacity for love. It grows out of your ability to accept your separateness as a person, appreciate the importance of existence itself, and embrace your reality. Imagine where these people are now. Upstairs? Pulling up the driveway at this minute?

(Pause)

Now conjure up the whole dreamscape, the people in the background, your new occupation or activity, the setting. Gather up as much of it as you can into a single image.

(Pause)

This dreamscape is you—the you that you are becoming. Its architecture, embellishments, and setting represent your physical and emotional needs as a human being and your most deeply felt dreams and goals. It is the direction in which you are taking your life. To maximize the benefits of this exercise, practice it consistently and frequently. Because there is no need to rebuild the structure every time you conjure up the image, it takes only a moment. You don't need to recite the four cornerstones. Just make sure that the way you've imagined the dreamscape takes each of them into account. You celebrate your separateness, the gift of existence, your reality, and your love capacity just by being contained therein.

The dreamscape gives your brain an energetic workout. To increase its benefits, you need to frequently imagine yourself engaging in productive future activities. Beyond activating your mirror neurons, your dopamine reward system, and your left prefrontal cortex, creating these visual images stimulates your brain's imagination factory—the parietal lobe—as well as other integrative areas including those involved in focus, problem solving, planning, and spatial calculation, to name a few. Given the brain's capacity to grow new neural connections, this exercise surely provides potent brain food. I recommend keeping your dreamscape on the screen of your mind throughout the day, and to imaginatively and actively return to it no less than three times a day for a few minutes at a time. Continue this for a period of three months (and beyond) to see real changes in your life. There is no need to close your eyes. You can revisit the image on the train or waiting at the post office.

As you identify new goals, renovate your dreamscape accordingly, so that it keeps up with (or stays ahead of) your current needs. Be prepared for forward locomotion. You are fast developing as a person; your needs are changing. You are fine-tuning your goals. You may decide to move your dreamscape to another country. Make it smaller or larger. Add a room or tear one down. Change your favorite spot from one room to another. Imagining these changes is good physical therapy for the brain. By renovating, you become a virtual architect. When you figure out the best place for a closet, staircase, new garden path, or orchard, you are unwittingly exercising your ability to solve parallel problems in real life. The more vivid the image, the better the mental workout. Many make a sketch of their dreamscapes to carry with them. Excellent! Remember, it's important to keep the image on your mind screen, and to actively imagine yourself within it at least three times a day.

Dreamscape taps into one of your most powerful resources—your imagination. Through it you become the engineer and architect of your own life. As the master designer, you create a safe, pleasurable place within, one that suits your greatest needs, goals, and desires. The dreamscape represents your true self and at the same time gives it a place to grow. It creates a positive sense of future. Visualizing your dreamscape embeds mindfulness and LovingKindness into an internal mental structure in which you can incubate love and move your life forward. What part of our mind does the building, designing, and problem solving involved in this exercise? My guess is that our wellspring of hope does the work of the visualization. This hope, though we may not feel it during abandonment, is deep within, ready to work for us, helping us break free from barriers like selfdoubt and over-people-pleasing. In our imagination, we are freed to discover the higher power within.

Where has this self been all of these years? As toddlers, when we were just beginning to discover the use of our limbs, we used them to venture away from our mothers and explore the world around us. Visualizing strengthens that incipient part of us that wants to explore, exercise its autonomy, experience freedom from the constraints of old relationships, and push forward into the future.

During the internalizing stage, we are in the heart of the self-injury process. We internalize feelings of rejection and anxiety about being alone. The internalizing energy is powerful. It acts like a centripetal force, pulling the feelings of rejection and desertion toward our centers, where our core beliefs are forged, where we silently judge ourselves unworthy or unlovable. When we were children and felt abandoned, we were less able to fight off self-doubts and anxieties, less emotionally resilient, and more easily wounded. We internalized feelings of rejection. We became afraid of being left alone.

As children, we erected makeshift barriers. We created internal gatekeepers to prevent hurt and fear from burrowing so deep. When we become adults, losing our love attachment wakes up the internal gatekeepers who have been secretly trying to keep life out all along. We feel everything keenly once again. We emerge from the ego wound, no longer choosing to doubt or devalue ourselves. It is time to internalize good feelings, to celebrate the gift of our own existence. Abandonment recovery beholds a vision that allows us to bypass the gatekeepers and rebuild with dreams, goals, acceptance, and love.

Internalizing brings us to a place deep within, where we wrestle the demons of doubt and fear. It is the soul's Gethsemane, from which we emerge with humility, strength, and vision.

STAGE FOUR: RAGE

Rage is a protest against pain. It is how we fight back, a refusal to be victimized by someone leaving us, the way we reverse the rejection. Those who know abandonment's rage know that its wound is tender, hot, and sore during this pivotal point of the healing process. We're agitated by nagging pain as we fight off toxins in the wound. Mending tissues are raw and taut. If anything comes near them, we cry out in anger. We are prepared for any threat, ready to defend against the subtlest criticism. Others may not realize the scope and depth of our wound. They brush up against it with no inkling of the pain they cause. We stand guard, protector of our emerging selves. We defend ourselves against further injury with the outer child. The outer child is the part of us that acts out our inner child's fear and rage. The outer child pretends to be our ally, our foot soldier, but it is really our gatekeeper. Its mission is to fight change and defend against feeling. It is during this fourth stage of abandonment that our defenses can become calcified. People may think they are strong again, but this outward show of strength is usually only the outer child becoming more firmly entrenched than before.

Controlling the impulses of our outer child is the key to true recovery. Learn to recognize its traits, and we can begin to dismantle our unhealthy defenses. Until now we have been doing the groundwork of healing; outer child work is the next task of recovery. We're changing our behavior. We all know that rage burns. It seethes and boils in the molten core of self. It also awakens the outer child—draws its maneuvering out in the open. Exposing the outer child is the turning point in the recovery process, the bridge to lasting change.

Roberta's Rage

Roberta vividly remembers the night she first noticed her mood turn from isolation to anger. She was getting ready to go to the symphony. She hadn't been inside a concert hall since she had caught Travis, the great maestro himself, with that other woman. She wished she had hit him harder, knocked him down with her bag and broken his nose. As far as she was concerned, he got off far too easily. But that was six months ago. Why should she be feeling so riled up about going to a concert now? She had learned the role Travis demanded of her and performed it for years: Be there at the concert to witness the accolades and afterward, lavish him with praise. How had she put up with it so long? Now she was on her way to the symphony again, this time, in the anonymous role of spectator. Not that she had ever been more than a spectator in Travis's life—he just needed her to keep his voracious ego fed. He certainly never gave anything back to her. Instead, he had taken the last four years of her life, her best years, and she had nothing to show for them. She spent the last six months in pure hell trying to get over it. It was time to wash the whole miserable mess out of her hair. How did he create such turmoil in her life, anyway?

She said all of this to herself, standing in front of her mirror. She really shouldn't have agreed to go, but John had an extra ticket, and in a weak moment, the part of her that loved music had told John he couldn't let it go to waste. She agreed to go, thinking it was long overdue. But suddenly the thought of walking into the concert hall was definitely not something she relished. She hadn't been out with anyone for so long. Well, this wasn't a date. It was only John, a friend, someone she'd met at an abandonment recovery group. John was no Travis. Not that he wasn't pleasant-looking, but he was definitely not her type—just too basic, missing that . . . she couldn't quite put her finger on what. John better not have any ideas. No, she hadn't given him any mixed signals. They were just friends.

Then came the knock. "Flowers," she almost shouted as she saw John's offering. "Get them out of here." John stood blankly in the doorway. Roberta grabbed the flowers and stuffed them upside down in the wastebasket by the door.

"Roberta," said John.

"I'm just not ready for that," she said, surprised at herself for such a display of anger. She wasn't expecting to show this side of herself to John. She tried to regain control. "I'm just not in the mood. You should know that, John. Doesn't anybody understand?" She held her head in her hands. John stood still in the door frame. "Oh, just come in," she said. "Sorry about the flowers! I have no idea why I'm reacting like this." But they both knew what it was about. She had told John all about Travis, many times.

John reached in his pocket and handed the suddenly teary Roberta a tissue. "How's my eye makeup?" she asked, blotting her face, trying to regain her composure.

"You look good," said John.

"That's not what I mean," she said, angrily. "Are my eyes smudged? Do you want me to go to a concert looking like a basket case?"

He handed her another tissue. "Roberta, if you don't like . . . we don't have to go," he said.

"No, let's go," she snapped, and grabbing up her purse, she slammed the door behind them.

The fourth stage of abandonment, rage, is the most volatile. The night Roberta went to the concert with John, her anger spilled over the edges of her wound. She had not yet learned how to harness her anger. In her case, it's easy to sense the grief and loneliness lurking just behind her anger. Notice that her anger is directed outward, rather than at herself. This represents progress from the self-rage that we saw during the internalizing process. Roberta feels a more effective, self-empowering type of anger that we begin to feel during this fourth stage. In Roberta's case, the transition from victim rage is not yet complete. She has not yet learned to channel the anger in a positive direction, and she displaces it upon an innocent bystander—John.

Sometimes we cycle through the five stages of abandonment so rapidly that we experience them almost simultaneously. Sometimes the process takes just minutes, sometimes it stretches over months. We know we're cycling through the rage process when our anger takes on a momentum of its own. Rage comes in emotional surges that leave us irritable and edgy. Sometimes a surge is explosive.

Losing our keys can send us into a blind fury. In fact, any loss or personal slight, real or imagined, can cause an unexpected eruption. After the isolation of the internalizing process, the fact that we can express anger is a good sign. It signifies active resistance to the injury. Rage tells us that the beleaguered self, under siege from self recrimination, is ready to stand up and fight back. As the self is no longer willing to take all of the blame, our rage must find outward release. Our anger begins as an impotent protest. We strike out at inanimate objects like pillows, but as we gain strength, it becomes more directed. We use its energy to break through the barriers of isolation. Rage insists upon righting the injustice and restoring your sense of self-worth. We can apply many of the "R" words characteristic of this turnaround to Roberta's scene with John. Through her anger she is starting to reverse the rejection and remove Travis from his pedestal. Her return to the concert scene is an attempt to reclaim her territory and relinquish her painful attachment. Difficult as it is, she's ready to make her reentry into the world.

Turning the energy behind your rage outward is not always a smooth process. It begins in fits and starts. Despite its turbulence, feeling and expressing rage is a necessary part of recovery. It is an active protest against injury that demands change. It helps us to start functioning again. "I thought I was really losing it," said Marie. "I didn't know whether to cry or scream. I had trouble coping with everything. At work, I had no patience at all. When teachers see students behaving the way I was, we call it 'low frustration tolerance.' Suddenly, the term applied to me. Everyone thought I had taken a turn for the worse. But it turned out that I was finally coming to terms with the changes in my life—and the hard work I had ahead of me to get back on track." In its raw form, rage is unrefined aggression. We act without thinking, yet we feel justified. Rage maintains an internal dialogue that feeds on itself and fans its own flames. It becomes defensive aggression when we perceive a personal attack and use rage to protect ourselves. Rage becomes offensive aggression when it is used to perform destructive acts of retribution. Rage can be both destructive and constructive. Your task is to transform its energy into healthy self assertiveness— that is, to take positive actions on your own behalf.

In the throes of rage, it was hard for me to believe that the turbulent mix of emotions I felt could possibly lead to peace or tranquility. But I'd seen that this aggressive energy served a purpose in the lives of the abandonment survivors I'd worked with. I knew that the agitation I was feeling was life calling me out of my self-imposed isolation. It meant that relief was just around the corner. This chapter will guide you through the forms that your anger can take during this stage. By the end, you'll be able to recognize anger's many functions and redirect its energy for your benefit. Later, I'll help you identify the unique characteristics of your outer child. Identifying outer child behaviors focuses your attention on the impact of your old losses. Now is the time to address that unfinished business, focus on where you may be stuck in anger, and break patterns of behavior that hold you back.

Rage is a time of power surges and blown emotional circuits that plague us at many points throughout the abandonment process. Rage maintains an internal dialogue that feeds on itself and fans its own flames. It seethes beneath the surface. Until we recognize our outer child, we act without thinking. We use our anger to justify our behavior. But there is a way to use our rage energy constructively. Constructive rage does not destroy, inflict injury, or perpetuate pain. It does not retaliate. It converts to healthy aggression. It is the energy we need to rebuild ourselves and our relationships. Baby steps allow us to break through Outer Child's post-traumatic hypnosis and repetition compulsions. Discovering the outer child transforms what had been a two-dimensional dialogue into the three dimensional framework we need to get unstuck. We get to choose our actions rather than be guided by habit and reenact deeply entrenched patterns. The deconstruction of the outer child holds the key to true recovery.

STAGE FIVE: LIFTING

Lifting is a time of hope. It is spontaneous remission. It starts slowly and gathers momentum. You've climbed to the top of the hill. You can see where you've been and where you're going. You've lifted above the turbulence of rage, disarmed the outer child defenses, and found the way out of self-defeating patterns. So far, your recovery has been focused on your needs, fears, and defenses. During lifting you begin to nurture relationships with others. Abandonment has awakened the child within. You've now comforted that child and cared for its long-neglected needs and feelings. No longer covered under layers of defenses, these needs and feelings are the bridge to greater love.

Holly's Lifting

Holly went on a blind date with a man someone at work had arranged. She fretted about how things would go. It was her first date in over a year. She wanted him to be impressed by her mature, cheerful attitude. She wanted him to see her as independent. She couldn't let him pick up any signs of desperation. She'd keep her loneliness out of sight. They went to a movie, then to the diner. Holly chatted about her life, about her volunteer work on the hotline. She tried to talk like someone who was happy and fulfilled. He seemed interested, but she could never tell for sure. She wondered what he might be feeling about her but cast those thoughts aside. What if he picked up what she was thinking? That was Tuesday. Today was Sunday, and still no text. She got up and pulled on a sweatshirt to go for a run. She had to get away from the thought that she was being rejected again. Four miles later, she arrived at a bookstore, her favorite destination. She decided to buy a book and spend the rest of her Sunday afternoon reading. She'd be in good form when it was time to show up at the restaurant for work at five.

Keaton's Lifting

Keaton awoke to birds chirping outside his window. Sunday morning, he thought, should I bother getting up? This same time last year, he would have spent a morning like this with Gabby shopping at the nursery for something to add to their garden. He was no longer interested in gardening, not without Gabby. But he did want the Sunday paper. Why not walk down to the store to breathe the fresh spring air? he thought. Then maybe later he'd get some of that laundry done.

He was surprised to see how many flowers were in bloom. The beauty of brilliantly colored tulips made him think of Gabby, and he briefly felt the tug of loss. But soon he found himself enjoying the gentle breeze. In town he noticed Holly. He knew her from the abandonment recovery workshops he attended. Something she'd said a few weeks ago stuck with him. He wanted to talk to her about it, but she always dashed out when the workshop ended or became engrossed in a conversation with someone else on her way out the door. Tucking the paper under his arm, he headed across the street to find her. During his next session with me he described his attempt to reach out to her. "Holly," he'd said coming up behind her, "how are you doing?" She seemed surprised.

"I was just grabbing the paper. Saw you and thought I'd say hello. How's it going?"

Her hair was pulled back in a ponytail. "Great," she said. "How's it going for you, Keaton?"

"Pretty good. Beautiful out, isn't it?"

"It is," agreed Holly.

"What are you doing with yourself?"

"Well, right now, I'm here to get a book."

Keaton paused. "Did you go on that blind date this week?"

"Yes."

"How did it go?"

"It went fine," she said, pulling a book off the shelf.

"Good," said Keaton. "You planning to see him again?"

No answer.

None of my business, Keaton thought. "Do you have some time? We could walk down to the water and talk."

"I'm not sure," said Holly. "But okay."

They slowly made their way two more blocks to the bagel shop and sat down at a table outside. Lifting is best described with "L" words. We lift out of the grief and back into life. We experience moments of levity, a lightness of mood and spirit, even as the memory of our lost relationship echoes through our thoughts. Life, in all of its fullness, begins to distract us from our sense of loss and personal injury. The grief has lessened, and we've left many emotional burdens behind.

For Keaton, the vibrant colors of spring reminded him of his loss. We can see that he was starting to let go of his obsessive thinking about Gabby and let life carry him forward. Lifting is what I call this final stage, but we have felt brief moments of lifting throughout the healing process. These momentary respites from grief lengthen to hours and then days as we enter the final stage.

For Holly, lifting involved a deliberate, self-directed effort. She chose to spend her day in positive, constructive ways—jogging, reading, and working—rather than focus on her disappointment over her date. Whether our elevated mood is spontaneous or, like Holly, we make a deliberate attempt to lift, it is during this stage that we move back into life. At times we feel like our old selves again; at others, we feel a whole new self emerging. Lifting is about new life; it is when we explore new territory, conquer new ground. We have been listening to important messages from within about our needs and feelings and learning from our painful experience. We are taking in new ideas about life and about ourselves and weaving them into new patterns of living. We discern who we are becoming. We let go of our rage toward the one who has left us, and we let go of old patterns as well. We know that the past still permeates our lives, but we discover that abandonment has brought us to a new place, that we are better off for what we have experienced.

One of the profound realizations of this stage is that we are getting ready to love again. It often begins with feelings of warmth and gratitude toward friends and family who were there for us in our time of despair. It is at this point that we find ways to let them know how important they are to us. We feel love and appreciation for ourselves as well, taking pride in the gains we've made. We're more self-reliant, self-aware, and open to our feelings. We feel our own capacity for love stirring within us as we reach out to make new connections. Lifting out of abandonment into greater life and love is the goal of this final stage, but it is important that when you lift, you take your feelings with you. One of the common pitfalls of the lifting stage is rising above your feelings, leaving your emotional center behind. You want to avoid this mistake, which can keep you at arm's length from intimacy in new relationships.

As I guide you through the final stage of abandonment, I will show you how you can use the energy of lifting to increase your capacity for life and love. This chapter carries messages of both triumph and caution. I will point out some stumbling blocks to forming relationships that are common to abandonment survivors and describe some of the ways they've learned to overcome them. I will review childhood scenarios that lead to the personality profile of the lifter and provide an inventory to help you identify some of the unfinished business left over from previous losses. Finally, I will introduce you to the fifth Akeru exercise designed to help you stay in touch with your feelings as you establish new quality relationships.

Lifting is a relief from insecurity, longing, and grief. It is a time to reflect upon the emotional truths revealed to us through our abandonment and take stock of the emotional baggage we have been carrying all along. This knowledge is gold, rich in personal wisdom. Lifting is the time to honor our feelings. If we can keep our emotional center open, its energy becomes self-generating, the impetus for continual healing—lifelong personal growth and connection.

As you integrate the exercises into daily practice over time, they begin to take on a less formal structure and become part of your everyday experience, incorporated into your actions and thoughts as positive habits. You are able to live in the moment, nurture your most important needs and feelings, reach for new goals, and respond to others as an adult. As you grow, your capacity for love grows with you.

CONCLUSION

Together, we have been on a journey through the five stages of abandonment. Along the way, our experiences often reminded us of earlier times. Becoming reacquainted with our oldest and most basic feelings has made us more self-aware. Abandonment opened us up to emotional truths and brought us in touch with universal life forces. It has been intense and powerful because we have been here before. Abandonment mirrors developmental stages we went through as children, as we made our way from infancy to the outside world.

In the shattering stage of abandonment, you were forced to survive the falling apart of a primary relationship and to re-enter the world in a state of stark separateness. Infants likewise must withstand the birth trauma, the jolt of being separated from the womb. In this first stage, then, both abandonment survivors and infants are forced to survive as separate individuals.

In the second stage of human development, infants form a bond with their caregivers to receive the nurturance they need for survival. In the second stage of abandonment, you experienced the same drive toward attachment, but the object of your attachment was no longer available. Your needs were thwarted, causing intense withdrawal symptoms. At stage two, both infants and abandonment survivors experience the powerful opioid-driven need for attachment.

In the third stage of human development, children internalize the sense of security they've gained through relationships with their parents. They transfer feelings of safety, trust and confidence onto their own newly forming sense of self. During the third stage of abandonment, you likewise internalized emotions, but the feelings you incorporated contained the message that you were unworthy. Like a young child, you transferred feelings derived from a primary relationship onto the self.

The fourth stage of human development is when children and adolescents, secure in the love and support of their family, feel confident enough to assert their place in the world. In the fourth stage of abandonment, called rage, you likewise returned to the external world, but you asserted the needs of your injured sense of self. In the fourth stage, both children and recovering adults move forward into the external world to meet their emotional needs. The difference is that you seek compensation for your injuries.

In the last stage of human development, emerging adults seek to form primary bonds. In the final stage of abandonment, lifting, you may experience the same desire to reconnect. But there is a need to protect yourself from further injury. In the fifth stage, then, young adults and those recovering from the loss of a love are propelled to form new attachments.

As an abandonment survivor, you gained valuable insight into the emotional baggage you carry forward into your relationships. Abandonment recapitulates the process of starting out in life; you retread all of its developmental stages. You've grown from infancy to adulthood all over again, this time as a fully conscious adult. You've created a new sense of self and perhaps set a new course for your life. You've converted the pain of abandonment into a milestone for personal change. Indeed, you have gained much from your experience.

AUTHOR BIO

SCOTT J. PINE

Scott J. Pine is an author and GP with years of experience as a health consultant.

After experiencing the deaths of his own parents and struggling to continue with life after the event, Scott began a long and arduous journey of healing in which he explored countless ways of dealing with grief and moving forward with life.

He discovered countless methods for practicing healing and coming to terms with his loss, and how he hopes to share them with others – offering them a profound roadmap for recovering from their own loss, practicing healing, and rebuilding their lives after the death of someone close to them.

Scott is the author of several other books, including *Loss of a Parent 2.0, Our Pets in Heaven* and *Attachment Theory And Couple Therapy 2.0.*

He lives in Oregon with his wife and three children.